"Raw food makes us healthy, reverses aging, and improves our appearance, and now you are holding in your hands the proof of raw food's value in rearing exemplary youth. On every page of this book, the authors will surprise and delight you with fresh insights and deep understanding into the child-parent relationship. Their intelligence is vivid, their wisdom is astute, and their love for others is stupendous. Whether you are a parent or child, you will gain insight from this book."

—**TONYA ZAVASTA**, author of *Your Right to Be Beautiful* and *Quantum Eating*

"Sergei and Valya share much wisdom and wit with sound nutritional guidance. They have been well taught and have a unique ability to share with others their perspective on the path to ultimate health."

—**BRIGITTE MARS**, author of *Rawsome!*, *Beauty by Nature*, *The Desktop Guide to Herbal Medicine*, and *Addiction Free—Naturally*

"Valya's and Sergei's new book inspires and encourages people to explore, persevere, and also to be courageous and imaginative with their new way of eating. They offer helpful and practical guidance and recipes that provide a foundation for success and enjoyment on a raw vegan diet."

—**VANCE M. LOGAN, MD**

fresh

fresh

THE ULTIMATE LIVE-FOOD COOKBOOK

Sergei and Valya Boutenko

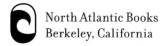

North Atlantic Books
Berkeley, California

Published by
North Atlantic Books
P.O. Box 12327
Berkeley, California 94712

Cover art by Robert Petetit
Cover and book design by Claudia Smelser
Printed in the United States of America on 30 percent recycled paper

Fresh: The Ultimate Live-Food Cookbook is sponsored by the Society for the Study of Native Arts and Sciences, a nonprofit educational corporation whose goals are to develop an educational and cross-cultural perspective linking various scientific, social, and artistic fields; to nurture a holistic view of arts, sciences, humanities, and healing; and to publish and distribute literature on the relationship of mind, body, and nature.

North Atlantic Books' publications are available through most bookstores. For further information, visit our Web site at www.northatlanticbooks.com or call 800-733-3000.

LIBRARY OF CONGRESS CATALOGING-IN-PUBLICATION DATA

Boutenko, Sergei.
Fresh : the ultimate live-food cookbook / by Sergei & Valya Boutenko.

    p.   cm.

Summary: "Featuring over 250 recipes, this is the first cookbook to run the gamut from casual brunch menus to high-end dinner entrées and is a fresh, new offering of live-food delights from the second generation of worldwide raw experts, Valya and Sergei Boutenko."—Provided by publisher.
ISBN 978-1-55643-708-3
1. Cookery (Natural foods) 2. Raw foods. I. Boutenko, Valya. II. Title.
TX741.B63 2008
641.5'63—dc22   2007042476

3   4   5   6   7   8   9   10   UNITED   15   14   13   12   11   10   09

To Nic and Lily

Acknowledgments

We would like to acknowledge Victoria and Igor Boutenko for educating us and giving us the proper tools to make up our own minds about health; Robert Petetit for being the friend who is always up for a late-night photo shoot; Allyson Holt of Allyson's of Ashland for lending us kitchen utensils; and our editors Aletha Nowitzky, Vanessa Nowitzky, and Rhoma Creary for their careful efforts.

Foreword

As an author and teacher of raw culinary arts, I am keenly aware of the many books on raw foods. Many contain excellent recipes for special occasions, while others focus on easy-to-prepare meals for every day. Some extol the healing benefits of raw foods, focusing on the relationship between diet and health, and often include first-hand stories of remarkable personal transformation. *Fresh* does all of this and much more.

Sergei and Valya Boutenko's heartfelt accounts of their experiences as young people caught in a web of disease while craving to be healthy—as well as dealing with the pressure of their peers—are both insightful and inspiring. In a refreshingly candid down-to-earth style all their own, this brother and sister team shares wise-beyond-their-years insights into the minds of young people and the many challenges encountered when choosing to eat only uncooked, unprocessed foods. They offer strategies for coping with the stresses of everyday life and staying with the raw diet even when friends and medical experts advise otherwise. These perspectives can help adults and youth alike understand why we find it so difficult to choose the foods that we know nourish us best.

In *Fresh* we visit the late-twentieth-century Boutenko family home through the children's eyes, learning how desperately this now-famous "raw family" fought to regain the health and well-being that so deftly eluded them in those early days. We read how these courageous siblings released excess body weight; improved their grades in school; and became free, happy, and purpose-filled young adults with the help of raw foods and the active, awakened lifestyle that accompanies them.

Many of us are succumbing to life-threatening diseases and looking for answers that cannot be found in a bottle. We are tired of being tired and sick of being sick. We want to reclaim our vitality and live a full and joyful life. Yet, for the first time in recorded history, our children are expected to have a shorter life span than their parents! Obesity, which is the cause of many life-threatening illnesses, is now epidemic in the Western world, and something needs to be done to stop it *now!* Unless they change their course, children raised on devitalized fast foods simply don't stand a chance of living up to their full potential as thriving, radiant, productive adults. Most will lack vitality and drive, endure depression and poor self-esteem, and suffer from a daunting list of debilitating and utterly unnecessary lifestyle-caused diseases.

Fresh proposes a simple, natural solution to this pervasive dilemma: fresh, organic, plant-based foods prepared without heating or processing. That means raw fruits and vegetables—in abundance! In *Fresh*, Sergei and Valya share some of their favorite, people-pleasing dishes with you. Their style of food preparation is innovative, yet deeply rooted in nature. They wrote this book for ordinary people who have little time to devote to making elaborate meals but want to enjoy the sensory pleasures of food while nourishing their bodies and becoming more fully alive. The majority of their 250 no-nonsense recipes use just a few ingredients, most of which can be acquired anywhere, and the dishes can be made in minutes. The directions are so easy that a child could follow them—and that is exactly the point!

Fresh is a very important book, and Sergei and Valya Boutenko are powerful and positive forces in this world. Children and young adults will readily identify with the perspectives of these two remarkably seasoned and engagingly authentic young people, and parents will welcome their positive, life-affirming message. Sergei and Valya shine as living examples of what is possible when we resolve to squeeze every drop of juice out of life. I know of no other book that can benefit both young people and their families as much as *Fresh*.

> —Cherie Soria, founder and director of Living Light Culinary Arts Institute and author of *Angel Foods: Healthy Recipes for Heavenly Bodies* and *The Raw Food Diet Revolution: Feast, Lose Weight, Gain Energy, Feel Younger!*

Contents

ONE

Raw Immersion

Dare to Prepare!

SERGEI: Often, when teaching food preparation classes, I notice that most of my students cling to recipes and request exact proportions of ingredients. Even though raw-food recipes are particularly flexible and experimentation can even improve the recipe, students still hesitate to take a playful approach with food preparation. For example, when I demonstrate how to make a green smoothie, I often use a combination of spinach, mango, and water, because these ingredients are readily available and excitingly delicious. However, in one workshop I was unable to find these ingredients and had to substitute with bananas and kale. My students loved the smoothie and requested the recipe. I made a point to mention that there are tastier recipes for a green smoothie; however, it seems my words fell on deaf ears, because months later I still received e-mails from people who, in fear of trying anything new, exclusively drank the banana/kale smoothie. To my surprise, most of my students did not stray from that recipe. While I can understand the fear behind attempting something new (there's the chance of wasting time and ingredients, and getting unsatisfying results), raw recipes allow much room to experiment, often improving the dish.

Every individual—whether man, woman, or child—is an amazingly powerful being, capable of happiness and health. We were built with a brain, a fabulous body, and an intuition to use as tools that aid us in our growth. When properly used, these tools have the power to enhance an individual's existence in the best, most productive way. We are not taught early enough how to use what we were given, which is why we cling to rules, regulations, and expert opinions. As with any tangible, physical tool that can be held in our hands, our intangible, invisible instruments cannot help us unless we begin to use them. I propose that, together, we begin activating these powers; for they are our maps to life.

There are certain laws that we need to follow to maintain order in our lives. Likewise, there are many that can be disregarded. Changing a recipe a bit doesn't hurt anyone. By adding one extra pinch of cumin to make a better-tasting cracker, we can practice conversing with our inner selves, thereby expanding our comfort zones. I have found that the more I experiment, the more comfortable I become with using my invisible tools, and thus the more empowered I become.

We live in a society that has either forgotten the value of empowered people or simply strives to suppress individuals from manifesting their strength. Today's society is so destructive that people no longer feel strong or comfortable enough to rely on themselves. Our educational system has us convinced that we cannot function successfully without help from authority figures. The current educational system grabs children at an early age and begins educating them to properly conform and comply with orders from people who are older, smarter, and more experienced than they. Instead of helping our children develop a sense of independence, we hand them off to their first kindergarten teachers and instruct them to listen to the educator because he or she has many years of training and therefore knows best. Thus, we come to learn that our bones cannot be strong without milk or healthy without meat, and that chemical fertilizers enrich food quality, as well as countless other myths that we cling to until our dying days.

If we live our lives believing that we are incapable of creating even a simple raw recipe on our own, then how can we do anything that requires more responsibility? I remember one instance when I was scheduled to demonstrate how to make carob truffles but was notified moments before class that none of my recipe ingredients had been delivered. I quickly ran to the kitchen, grabbed whatever I could find, and proceeded to demonstrate making truffles with ingredients I had never used before. My heart pounded anxiously as I passed out samples to a crowd of fifty, hoping my concoction didn't taste horribly bad. To my surprise, the room resonated with audible *yum*'s and *wow*'s. Everyone was ecstatic. The "Sweet and Sour Coconut Truffles" recipe I invented that day is in the dessert section of this book (page 111). However, don't let this recipe limit your imagination.

Relying on yourself is fun and refreshing! The more I rely on myself, the more surprised I am at not only how easy it is but also how quickly I master things I never suspected I could. I encourage you to use the recipes in this book merely as a guide to creating your own cuisine.

HOW WE CAME TO EAT RAW FOOD

I was diagnosed with diabetes at the age of nine. Our family doctor informed my parents that unless I immediately began taking insulin shots, my health would deteriorate and possibly become unsalvageable within months. The doctor said that having such high blood sugar could cause a coma and even death. My world crumbled as I dived into self-pity, a state of mind that brought me misery and pain. Thoughts such as "Why me?" and "What did I do to deserve this?" overwhelmed me without end. No longer was I going to be a normal boy! I was to carry my disability until the day I died, which unfortunately appeared to be a lot sooner than I had hoped.

All of a sudden, my family's health took a definite turn for the worse. My mother was diagnosed with arrhythmia and told to either find a way to lose 120 pounds or be prepared to die suddenly at any time. Due to hyperthyroid, my father was given two months to live and told that if he survived longer, arthritis would put him in a wheelchair by the end of the year. I remember how terrified I was when I became aware of the seriousness of the situation. In horror I wondered which parent I would lose first and what it would be like to live the rest of my life with such a loss. At night, I could hear my little sister suffocating from repeated asthma attacks while she slept. The real shock came when my mother found me unconscious on the bathroom floor. My mother hesitated to place me on insulin, despite pressure to do so right away from doctors who threatened to call social services and have my sister and me taken away. Because her grandmother had died of an insulin overdose, my mother knew that a person could never take an accurate amount of insulin (too much or too little is always administered), which eventually takes its toll on the diabetic's eyesight , organs, and extremities.

It was clear to us that going the medical route was futile. Doctors did not promise us any hope of wellness. The cures for most illnesses are unknown. What does this mean? It means that doctors prescribe remedies that they know will not work. In desperation, my mother began to search for an alternative. As she hunted through the abundant world of medicine in hopes of finding a natural way to manage diabetes, we began experimenting with different diets, such as Slim-Fast, vegetarianism, macrobiotics, Ayurveda, eliminating sugar, reducing meat and dairy consumption, and eliminating wheat, but nothing worked. On the rare occasion when I stumbled onto something that actually affected my blood sugar levels, it either proved fruitless in the long term or did not provide the results I sought. All medical, nutritional, and standard and alternative health books claimed that diabetes was incurable. I remember seeing my mother sitting in the kitchen with her head in her hands, crying before a plethora of open books with the words *incurable, cure not found,* or *irreversible* highlighted. "How can this be?" she asked me in bewilderment. I couldn't respond. It seemed hopeless.

After discovering that books held few answers, my mother began asking healthy-looking people on the street what they did to stay vibrant. One day, while standing in a bank line, she asked a radiant older lady standing in front of her what she knew about health. The woman, whose name was Elizabeth, responded that she ate "raw foods." She told my mother that she had cured herself of colon cancer fifteen years earlier by changing her diet. When my mother asked her if she thought diabetes could be reversed naturally, her answer was, "Of course!" Elizabeth explained that heating food over 118 degrees destroys vital nutrients and enzymes that are necessary to maintain health.

Several days later, my mother cleaned out our kitchen, threw away the microwave, and covered the stove with an enormous cutting board. Knowing we had no time to lose, she had us change our diets overnight from a standard American diet of fast food, dairy products, meat, starches, refined flour and sugar, cooked carbohydrates, and refined oils (with occasional salads) to a raw, vegan diet consisting of fruits, vegetables, greens, nuts, seeds, sprouts, and berries.

The first day was miserable. Food we were no longer allowed to eat seemed to be on every channel on TV, in every book, and on the cover of every magazine. Our kitchen was haunted by the memories of delicious food. Oddly enough, the next day everyone appeared to feel a little better. At first we thought this was simply coincidental, but day after day we showed unmistakable signs of improving health.

A week later, my sister and I had holes in all of our fingers from checking our blood sugar so regularly. Although Valya did not have diabetes, our readings were becoming similar. My readings began to jump around less. I discovered that even sweet fruits did not make my blood sugar skyrocket and then plummet as refined sugars did. Valya had not had an asthma attack in seven days, and both of my parents were losing weight and feeling better. Slowly, we began regaining our health.

One day, during a routine blood sugar test, I charted the lowest figures I had observed since my diagnosis. Instead of reading 200 milligrams per deciliter (mg/dL), as it had read before I began eating raw foods, my blood sugar was in the normal range at 85 mg/dL. This excited me very much! Not only had I begun experiencing a physical calmness that would have been impossible with too much sugar in my bloodstream, but now I also saw actual scientific data that revealed progress in reversing diabetes. I monitored this phenomenon over the next few weeks and found that, though it fluctuated at times, overall my blood sugar was normal. I felt drastically better! My blood sugar readings continued to stabilize until I got perfect readings in my blood glucose monitor every time!

It has now been fourteen years since we started eating raw foods in 1994. My mother lost 120 pounds and got rid of her arrhythmia, my father was liberated from both his hyperthyroid and arthritis, and from the day she changed her diet, my sister Valya never suffered from another asthma attack. My diabetes vanished without a trace. After getting perfect readings every time for months on end, I sold my blood glucose monitor to my math teacher for five dollars. I have learned that a wretched curse and a blessing are only distinguished by one's perception. Getting sick, overcoming my illness, and sharing what I have learned about health with the world has been nothing short of a precious gift. Sometimes people who don't believe my story come to my house and demand to check my blood sugar for themselves. Much to their amazement, my readings are always within the normal range.

Along with our major illnesses, all the small signs of poor health went away as well. Our teeth and fingernails became stronger, my mother's eyesight improved, and the pain in her feet went away. Because she had constantly had extremely dry, deeply cracked skin on her hands, she had always worn bandages around her fingers. Lotions had never seemed to help. We had always thought that this condition was from doing too many dishes. My sister and I even attempted to take over that duty, but this didn't help either. However, when we changed our diets, my mother's skin became smooth within weeks and has not reverted since. My father's hair stopped falling out, regrew in places, and got darker near the temples where it had started turning gray. My skin became clearer, and I lost the extra weight I had carried. Both my sister and I had an easier time concentrating, and we all had more energy.

We live in a time when being unhealthy is considered the norm. It wasn't until I became healthier that I realized how sick I had been and in fact how unhealthy most everyone else still was. Strangely, if you had asked me before I changed my diet whether I considered myself healthy, I would have answered, "Yes!" with assurance. It has become clear to me that the majority of ailments people live with every day are totally unnecessary. Our bodies are made to remain healthy throughout our lives, from beginning to end. When presented with the opportunity, our bodies begin to repair themselves.

I once got a phone call from a woman who was selling insurance and wanted to know if my family spent thirty dollars or more per month on medications. I said, "No, we don't." There was an odd pause at the other end, and then the woman responded in a slightly strangled tone, "You are very lucky," and hung up the phone.

I have come to believe that every person, young or old, is entitled to be healthy. This well-being is our birthright and can be maintained until old age. Somewhere in time we lost the sense that feeling good physically, mentally, and spiritually was aimed at everyone. With all the organic fresh foods and information available today, our health has never been more accessible, attainable, realistic, and, best of all, even free.

VALYA:

How Clarity of Mind Is Influenced by Diet

I would not interfere with any creed of yours
Or want to appear that I have all the cures.
There is so much to know. . . . So many things are true . . .
The way my feet must go may not be best for you. . . .
And so, I give this spark of what is light to me,
To guide you through the dark but not tell you what to see.
Unknown Author

I was blessed by the curse of asthma. Having this illness and overcoming it has taught me that my response to life is what determines my fate. The idea that there are thousands of vicious diseases hiding in the bushes waiting to attack and kill me is, at best, a bogus illusion. Being healthy is each person's own responsibility. For me, choosing a responsible life does not mean being *independent* from the world but realizing the implications of being *interdependent*. Everything we do affects the rest of the world. For example, researchers studying the extinction of polar bears tested the blood of a newborn polar bear and found it laden with man-made chemicals, some of which were traced to DDT and other common pesticides.[1] After discovering this, I felt even more compelled to eat organic produce. In the words of Marshall Rosenberg, "One cannot meet his own needs at the expense of another."[2] The freedom I feel from living a nondestructive life is empowering. In taking care of myself, I care for the world; and in taking care of the world, I care for myself.

I know that the way I interact with the world has changed due to the way I eat. When I changed my diet, I regained my health on many levels, but what stood out most was an intense shift in mental clarity. It was as though a fog had cleared or a veil had been lifted. Right away, my school studies improved drastically. I went from being a poor student to an A student in a matter of months. All of a sudden, I found myself able to concentrate whenever I needed to, for as long as I needed. I felt that every subject had become available to me and that there was *nothing* I could not learn. I stopped waiting for my teachers to "teach" me something, as if it were up to them to educate me, and began to educate myself. At the same time, the majority of my fellow third graders still had trouble focusing. It was difficult for them to simply sit still. They experienced the mood and energy swings that were all too familiar to me.

When I changed my diet, I began to enjoy reading. I even started to prefer reading to watching television. Pretty soon I was reading a book a day. After one summer vacation, we were asked to bring a list of the books we had read during the break. When it was my turn to share with my class the books I had read, turning slightly pink, I pulled out a scroll. Because my list of books had grown, I had to staple several sheets of paper together, and now the paper reached the floor.

I don't think I'm better or smarter than anyone else. I do believe that mental clarity is directly linked to diet. I have heard similar stories from many other students who performed dramatically better in school after implementing dietary changes. My enhanced mental ability has drawn me to question the very idea of intelligence as we know it.

After taking an IQ test at school, I noticed a dangerously detrimental misapprehension about the nature of intelligence. For many educators and students, it appeared that intelligence was not only measured by, but equated with, knowledge. I believe this to be an entirely false assumption, because knowledge is only the by-product of a curious mind. It is not how much we know but, rather, how much we *want* to know that determines the brightness of our minds. I believe that curiosity is intelligence in its purest form. For example, you do not know whether I am right- or left-handed. If I tell you that I am in fact right-handed, you have acquired some knowledge about me, but have you become smarter? No. The distance between knowing and not knowing is virtually nonexistent. In this case, what determines your intelligence is the intensity with which you peruse the information, which in turn stems from how much you wanted to know. At school, I found that people believed themselves to be "bad" at things they knew nothing about! Students repeatedly made the insane assumption that not understanding something right away equaled stupidity. This simply isn't so! How quickly people catch on to things depends a great deal on the strength of their long- or short-term memory. Although it takes more repetitions to store information in long-term memory, the information stored there will be accessible much longer than in short-term memory! On the other hand, those students who immediately catch on to new subjects often do not retain their newly acquired knowledge for very long. I have watched my fellow students carefully skirt around subjects they had never even tried to learn, fearing that others would discover their "lack of intelligence."

I do not believe that we are predisposed to be awful at certain subjects, and would even argue that we can become better at the things that are difficult for us than the things that come easily due to the inexorable determination that can be ignited by opposition. Personally, I think the excitement of pursuing something at which everyone is convinced you will fail surpasses the pleasant social approval of talent. Our flaws and weaknesses generate compassion, love, kindness, and generosity, because they enable us to relate to the suffering of others. Vulnerability is the backbone of every revered human quality. Therefore I question whether it is our talents or inadequacies that are responsible for our virtues.

Eating healthfully did not raise my IQ, but it cleared my thinking processes (thereby inspiring an insatiable curiosity) and gave me the energy necessary to follow my ever-expanding interests.

I entered college at the age of fourteen. Something I immediately noticed on campus was that people related to each other through complaints. The most common thing to complain about was health. It actually took me a while to learn how to fit in with my college peers, because I often found it difficult to relate to their pain since I felt well the vast majority of the time. The following is one of the countless typical conversations I had with other students:

Me: "Hey."

Henry: "Hey."

Me: "How are you?"

Henry: "Man, I puked all over everything I own last night, I'm running on three hours of sleep, and my head feels like it's a ticking time bomb about to go off."

Me: "Uh, that's great."

Henry: "You?"

Me: "I'm actually feeling pretty rested today."

Henry: "I'm behind in everything. Do you understand anything the teacher is saying?"

Me: "Yes."

Henry: "That party was crazy last night."

Me: "That it was."

Henry: "I feel so bad; I hate school so much. I just want to be done."

Me: "I feel really good today. It's fascinating that mass divided by volume equals density. I love knowing that water has the density of 1 and ice has the density 0.9, and that ice is only ten percent lighter than water, which is why we only see the tip of the iceberg (the ten percent that is lighter than water)."

Henry: "Wow, that's interesting. Where did you learn that?"

Me: "In the earth science class we just had together."

Henry: "Oh. Heh-heh." (He starts walking away.) "See ya later."

Me: "See ya."

At first, students found me strange and stopped talking to me, but pretty soon I figured out that all people wanted when they complained was some compassion. They even preferred this to my trying to outdo them at suffering. After that, I no longer felt that I had to relate to their experiences to communicate with them. I simply tried to picture myself in the other person's place and respond genuinely, with comments such as, "That must be very unpleasant." Several students even began calling just to tell me what was going on in their lives. What stood out to me was how tired they always seemed. While I felt that I always had a surplus of energy I could rely on, my peers constantly complained of exhaustion. I wondered how they managed to do all they did.

It makes me sad to think of the possibility that perfectly intelligent students might be labeled as slow or dyslexic, or as having attention deficit/hyperactivity disorder (ADHD) simply from dietary imbalances! I am not saying that these things don't exist but merely that learning disabilities may not be as permanent as they are thought to be and that this type of labeling alone could be enough to make a person give up on certain feats or interests. Instead of looking forward to the opportunities presented by challenges, this kind of categorizing acts as a barricade that limits one's abilities. The first time I took drawing in college, I was by far the worst student in the class. I got a C, even though I did all of my homework and never missed class. It was this very event that encouraged me to major in art. Three years later, when I took drawing again, my teacher asked me if I wanted to switch my emphasis from ceramics to drawing because she thought I was "talented."

Our interests are clues into the heart of who we are. They lead us in search of an unnameable happiness and satisfaction. I meet people who postpone their dreams their entire lives, never really living for themselves, always too busy to do what they want and needlessly denying themselves the manifestation of their dreams. This pattern leads to an unfortunate disappointment in life. But it is never too late. In every moment we are given the opportunity to change. Why shouldn't you get what you want? Why are we taught that desire is wrong? Through repression, desires can become contorted, but in their purest form, they are benevolent. If a desire seems dark, there is usually a real need underneath it. For example, the desire for power can secretly be a desire for approval, which is often the need for self-approval. It is not natural for us to want to hurt one another.

I believe that in spite of all historical evidence to the contrary, human nature is compassionate. I came to this conclusion one day when I went to see a sad movie by myself. Halfway through the film, I heard some sniffling behind me, so I slid down in my seat and peeked over my shoulder. There were tears streaming down the cheeks of many audience members. I myself had a hard time holding back tears when I saw how moved these people were by the troubles of the strangers on the screen. When the unexpected happy ending took place, the faces of the people in the theater softened into angelic smiles that are too infrequently seen in the daylight. It was remarkable that all of these different people showed such vulnerable emotions when they thought they were not being watched and judged for it. At the end, when the audience stood up to leave, many of them once more took on a serious demeanor.

While acquiring a minor in psychology, I learned that the leading group to attempt suicide was college-age males.[3] This did not surprise me. Depression was rampant on my college campus. What did surprise me was how receptive students were to the idea of eating more healthfully. Quite frequently, as I walked from one class to the next, someone with an excited grin who recognized me from my family's books would run up beside me and breathlessly begin to tell me that he or she had begun eating a raw-food diet and started having fewer headaches, shinier hair, and so on.

Sometimes my professors had read about my family and asked me to speak in front of their classes. At these times, my main message was that *our* health is in *our own* hands. I once spoke about an intriguing psychological experiment I had read about. This is how it went: Imagine that you enter a room to take what you believe to be a simple eye test. When you arrive, there are eight people already seated at a large table. You take the last empty seat. All you have to do is determine which of two straight lines is longer. This is pretty easy to do. For the first few rounds, everyone gives the correct answer, but eventually everyone except you begins to give the incorrect answer. They begin to say that the shorter line is actually the longer one. What are you going to do? Is your vision failing you? Have you lost your mind? How can everyone give the wrong answer? What you don't know is that the wrong answer is given on purpose and that this experiment is designed to test conformity levels. Thirty-seven percent of the time, subjects consciously gave the wrong answer, trusting that others knew better than they did.[4] Interestingly, having at least one other person in the room give the right answer reduced conformity by eighty percent.[5]

What about situations when it is not as easy to determine the correct answer? What if the entire world says that humans need to eat cooked food, but you can see that there is not one other animal on this planet for which this is also a requirement? It takes great courage to hold true to one's own observations under pressure. From time to time, my cousin Katya gets migraine headaches. I asked her if she ever took medication to ease the pain. She told me that she had once bought some aspirin but decided against taking it after reading about its potential side effects, which included damage to the stomach lining, stomach bleeding, ringing in the ears, hearing loss, prolonged bleeding time, wheezing, breathlessness, chronic catarrh and runny nose, *headache*, confusion, nausea, vomiting, gastric upset and or bleeding, ulcers, rashes, hives, bruising, abnormal liver functions, liver damage, hepatitis, kidney damage, respiratory and central nervous system damage, and strokes; fatal hemorrhages of the brain, spleen, liver, intestines, and lungs; and even death![6] I think this is a good example of a person trusting her own logic.

Ignorance is *not* bliss; it has people all over the world asking the painful question, "Why me?" The relief of knowing what's going on and what can be done about it is far more comforting than trying to escape facing difficult questions. The facts about nutrition are readily available, yet few can connect the dots. The perfect human diet has yet to be discovered. Isn't it strange that, unlike other, "unintelligent" life forms on earth, humans do not know what they should eat? This elementary aspect of our existence has been over-studied into a maddening array of contradictory information. Yet the truth is always right in front of us. But don't take my word for it, find out for yourself.

HOW Raw FOOD AFFECTS RELATIONSHIPS

SERGEI: Once, after teaching a raw food class, I met a woman who planned to leave her husband because of his unwillingness to try raw food. Despite having been on a raw food diet only a month, Wendy was tired of nagging her hubby and certain that he would never change. One year later, I received an e-mail from Peter, Wendy's ex-husband, who informed me that he was no longer with Wendy but was engaged to a new woman, with whom he shared a raw food lifestyle. Peter was excited about raw foods and asked whether my sister and I were available to cater his wedding. In the postscript of his e-mail, Peter mentioned that, ironically, Wendy no longer ate raw food. This is but one of many instances I have encountered where a dietary change affected a relationship. Although there are many benefits associated with a raw-food lifestyle, relationships can also suffer and fall apart due to dietary changes. It does not have to be this way!

With good communication and empathy, relationships can actually be improved and strengthened for years to come. *Merriam-Webster* defines the word *relationship* as "A state of affairs existing between those having relations or dealings," for example, with friends, family, or romantic partners.[7] To expand this definition, a relationship accounts for all of the interactions that we share, not only between ourselves and those closest to us but also with our acquaintances and coworkers. Poor communication can destroy our families and love lives, and also affect the people we work with or see on a regular basis, making our work environments unpleasant to be in.

Raw food comes to many of us as a miracle, making amends for the many years of poor habits that led us to a dead end. To maintain a raw food diet that will eradicate illness and allow optimal health, many of us are forced to resort to radical measures; for example, knowing that keeping pots and pans around the house would encourage fantasies of deep-fried Russian piroshkis and French toast, my mother made sure to throw them in a dumpster across town. She knew that, otherwise, in a moment of temptation, climbing into the garbage at home wouldn't be a problem for us.

Once we settle into our groove, we relax a bit, and our new lifestyle assumes a natural feel. Overwhelmed with new energy on top of good health, we begin to wonder why more people don't jump onto the bandwagon. Our health benefits compel us to share our stories, and somewhere along the way, we begin criticizing those close to us for their eating habits, what they feed their children, and even how they live their lives. As a result, friends part, couples divorce, families fall apart, and coworkers avoid each other in the workplace. I have been as guilty of this behavior as anyone else.

After healing myself of diabetes, losing weight, and getting a taste of true health, I was convinced that the raw way was the only way; I began my own ministry, preaching to anyone with ears. It didn't matter whether they cared to listen; I told them anyway, because I believed it was good for them to hear. I would see my friend Stephen eating french fries and, pointing my finger, yell, "Stephen, do you know what those death sticks are doing to your colon? They are lining your intestines with crap!" It was not long before he began expressing immense distaste for being on trial for his food choices. Needless to say, people will only put up with so much discomfort before they rebel. Within months, the majority of my friends, with the exception of Stephen, no longer wanted to associate with me. I feel fortunate that, at the time, my family was aligned with me in a commitment to raw food; for I fear that I would have lost them too because of my poor communication.

One day, approximately six months after I started eating raw food, I was humbled by a teammate during soccer practice. After informing me that I was fat, Nelson recommended that I lose extra pounds by running more frequently and farther than usual. I remember feeling so enraged that I decided to disregard his advice. After considering Nelson's rude words, I was determined to rebel and do just the opposite of what he had recommended. I would stop running altogether! This was when I had my epiphany: when I point out what others do wrong, maybe they, too, feel judged and react defensively. I finally understood that life has something different in store for each and every individual, and I have no place meddling and instructing others in matters I'm not sure about. I then asked myself one question that I still periodically ask myself, "Can I be one hundred percent certain what is best for me in the long run?" The answer was and is no! If I don't even know what's best for me, then how can I possibly know what's best for others?

From that day forward, I decided to stop convincing others. I started omitting any information about diet from conversations unless I was sure that my audience wanted to know. How could I be sure that someone wanted to know? I decided to reveal nothing unless I heard some phrase along the lines of "I am dying to know!" or "If you don't tell me, I will burst!" After all, I would rather save a life with a few words than see a friendship perish.

The root of why some relationships crash and burn while others get stronger is communication. Productive communication is not taught at an early enough age.[8] No matter what country you're from, the chances are almost nonexistent that your elementary school offered a class in "life-enriching communication," perhaps because, on the surface, communication seems so simple that, perceivably, there's nothing to teach. Marshall B. Rosenberg, author of *Nonviolent Communication: A Language of Love*, believes that, no matter what background they have, all humans are innately compassionate creatures. He writes that when engaging in communication with a fellow human, we face a fork in the road: one way leads to life-alienating communication—interactions laden with judgments, accusations, and blame—while the other route leads to understanding, acceptance, and forgiveness.[9] Whether discussing food choices or golfing, we must identify which type of communication we seek to achieve.

In preaching about raw food, I often chose the road of alienation. I now realize that I was not interested in accepting and loving people but simply wanted reaffirmation that my lifestyle was more enlightened. This kind of communication rarely led me to convince anyone that raw food was worth trying. It was not until I stopped concentrating on people's wrongdoings and started noticing their positive characteristics that I began rebuilding old friendships and acquiring new ones.

When I started college, I met my friend Seth. Seth and I shared an incredible passion for snowboarding, so we began keeping each other company on the slopes. It did not take Seth long to notice that our meals were different. At the ski lodge he often ordered fried food from the deli, while I had some trail mix, fruit, or nothing at all. Finally, one day he asked about my food choices. I assessed his desire to know and decided that he wasn't passionate about his inquiry. I told him that eating a heavy meal weighed me down and hindered my snowboard performance after lunch. This answer satisfied him and ended that particular conversation.

A few weeks went by, and Seth, who now regularly hung out with me, began to notice that my diet solely consisted of fresh fruits, veggies, nuts, and seeds. He asked again about my food choices. This time, I saw a sparkle of genuine curiosity in his eye. Just to be absolutely positive he was interested, I asked him, "How badly do you want to know?" He replied that he was *dying* to know!

I proceeded to tell Seth the story of how and why I came to eat raw food. The next time we went snowboarding, I was shocked to see Seth pull out dried mangoes and almond butter from his pack. Slightly discombobulated, I asked Seth why he wasn't ordering from the deli. Apparently he had noticed enough of a difference between his and my performances after lunch that he felt left out and wanted to give eating more healthfully a try.

Since that time, I have had many similar experiences. I must say that not only do I influence more people in this manner but also I take great pleasure in accepting others. Refraining from judging people causes them to relax, open up, and shine. People often confess to me that they feel comfortable eating anything around me because they do not feel judged. They also agree that this single fact, in itself, makes them more interested in trying raw food.

HELPING CHILDREN BECOME HEALTHIER

VALYA: Parents often ask me how they can make their children eat healthier. I tell them that they can't *make* their children eat healthier, but they can *inspire* them to want to eat more healthfully. It is not true that children don't want to be healthy. Everyone wants to be strong, clearheaded, and full of energy. Children claim that they dislike healthful food as a means of protecting themselves from being pressured to do something they don't want to do. If your children revolt at the idea of eating healthfully, it means they have a will of their own. It is a sign that they want to choose for themselves, and this is a blessing.

Problems occur when we want a child to want something he or she does not want. In this case, it is important to consider what we would like the reason for the child's action to be. Do we want our children to mindlessly obey our commands and the commands of others? Do we want them to do what we say out of fear of punishment? Or do we want our children to make decisions that are motivated by their own personal values?

In the words of Alfie Kohn, the author of *Punished by Rewards*, "Punishments and force produce only anger, defiance, and a desire for revenge. They encourage power over reason, and crush delicate relationships between children and parents."[10] Punishments can force a child to comply temporarily, but it's unlikely that such tactics will teach children to make better decisions in the future. When children know they will be punished for certain actions, they deal with the situation in the most logical way, which is to start lying about their behavior.

As Marshall B. Rosenberg writes in his book *Nonviolent Communication*, "I wonder whether people who proclaim the successes of punishment are aware of the countless instances of children who turn against what might be good for them simply because they choose to fight, rather than succumb to, coercion."[11]

So, what are we to do? How can we help our children become healthy? I have noticed that children are highly susceptible to inspiration. When kids are around my brother and me, they start eating more healthfully without our even mentioning raw foods. They can see for themselves how easy it is to eat healthful foods and how much fun it is to be healthy. As Krishnamurti once said, "To teach by example is not the *best* way to teach; it is the *only* way."[12] As parents, grandparents, and friends, you can be a great influence on children, inspiring them to make good choices. This does not mean that you have to be gung ho every instant of the day, hyping yourself up to appear excited, but rather that you exhibit a sincere personal interest and curiosity about health. Children can easily detect when adults are not being real with them, and quickly begin to mistrust those who appear insincere. Yet, they are drawn to those who are genuine with them. When an adult is authentically interested in something, as though it is his or her own venture, children begin to pay attention.

From years of babysitting, I have observed that children (especially young children from one to three years of age) can easily learn to love healthful food, as long as fruits and vegetables are made available to them. In fact, in my experience, many children prefer eating fresh blueberries as a snack instead of cheese and crackers. At such a young age, they have a very weak attachment to more-stimulating cooked foods, and can easily sustain themselves on healthy foods. My two-year-old nephew has been drinking green smoothies ever since he started eating solid foods. He is one of the healthiest babies in his age group in his city. When he wants a green smoothie, he points to the cupboard containing the Vita-Mix and yells, "VVVVVVV!" imitating the sound of the blender!

However, the more children are fed addictive foods, the stronger grows their dependency upon them. Cooked food provides overwhelming sensory stimulation.[13] The concentrated flavors and smells of cooked foods stimulate the nine-thousand taste buds on the tongue and 40 million olfactory receptor neurons in the nose, sending pleasure signals rushing to the brain.[14] Also, the body must cope with an enormous surge of unnatural substances to maintain its chemical balance (homeostasis) and continue to operate. If these substances are ingested daily, the body adapts to accommodate these stimulants and eventually depends upon them for maintaining homeostatic balance. "The removal of these foods will cause withdrawals. During withdrawal, the body suffers through a stressful readjustment as [it] cries out for the missing substance, attempting to attain homeostasis by demanding the very substance that caused the imbalance to begin with."[15]

Therefore, due to the addictive nature of cooked food, by the time children are five years old, they may no longer prefer eating healthfully, and are even likely to resist their parents' efforts to reform their diets. It is essential to remember that we were the ones responsible for helping our young friends establish their eating habits, and must therefore be gentle when trying to shift these patterns.

One of the most important things to do when introducing raw foods to children is to make it a positive experience. First impressions last forever, so it's a good idea to present children with something yummy, such as banana ice cream or mango walnut pie rather than wheatgrass juice or energy soup. In all my years of eating raw foods, not once have I met a child who didn't enjoy eating sweet fresh fruits. With some of the more difficult cases of wonderfully strongwilled children, it can be necessary to leave something scrumptious on the kitchen table, and leave the room. Upon your return, the treat has usually disappeared.

I first changed my diet at age eight. At first I ate mostly fruits without many vegetables. This is common for children. However, eventually they also develop a taste for greens and veggies, as I did. It is vital to make fresh fruits and vegetables available to them at all times. Here are some ideas for how you can support the habit of healthful eating:

- Leave delicious food on the table for the children to discover when they get home from school.
- Make green smoothies for breakfast or as a snack.
- Provide extra food to be shared with other children at school or social events.
- Substitute wholesome food for unhealthy treats at traditional social events; for example, make raw chocolates or carob balls to give to others for Valentine's Day.
- Give your children a raw cake to eat just before attending a friend's birthday party, so that their stomachs will be so full of heavenly tasting raw dessert that they won't even be tempted to eat the traditional nonnutritious party food.

- Hang pictures of fruits and vegetables on the walls, as well as charts about nutrition or exotic fruit and wild edibles.
- Plant a garden and have a vegetable stand during the summer.

Since eating healthy can be uncomfortable in social situations, communication plays a critical role in the success of changing the dietary habits of young kids. It is vital that children have someone to talk to who understands how they feel, someone who can reassure them that they are doing the right thing. Sometimes children have so regularly been told to sit still and be quiet that they are not sure how to communicate their true thoughts and feelings. In these situations, questions such as, "How was school?" are not enough to get them to disclose how they felt about the day's happenings. Anyone who was ever asked such questions knows that they do not demonstrate a desire to listen but, rather, support the appearance of caring communication without exerting the energy that real communication calls for. I have found that asking children questions that you yourself would like to answer works best. Here are some of my favorites:

- What is one thing that caught your attention today?
- What is something you heard that made you stop and think?
- What stirred you up or surprised you today?
- What made you sad?
- What lifted your spirits?

When asking these questions, it is important to put all else aside and really listen. Relate back to the child what you thought you heard him or her say to make sure you understood it.

For me, it was hard to be the only one in my entire school who ate raw foods. I was in the third grade when I changed my diet, and even my teachers did not understand the way I ate. I was faced with an entire world that disagreed with what I was learning about health. In the beginning I felt as though by eating my "freak" diet I was committing social suicide. I had made fun of the three vegetarians in my grade, and virtually overnight, I had surpassed them all in the spectrum of dietary extremes. At first I got away with hiding the fact that I ate avocados, bell peppers, and scallions for lunch every day. When my teachers asked where my sandwich was, I would simply say that I had already eaten it. I did not consider this a lie, because I had eaten it (long, long ago). Pretty soon, though, everyone did begin to notice, and for a while it was hard not to stand out, because eating healthfully was just about as uncool as eating your own boogers!

Children have been educated to hate nutritious foods. I think the idea that healthful foods taste disgusting was initiated by television advertisements of processed foods and reinforced by adults who grew up believing similar ads. In my elementary-school cafeteria, the only raw items available for lunch were non-organic rock-hard kiwis and mushy last year's apples that were so bland that the wax coating dominated their flavor. One day, as I stood in line waiting to enter the cafeteria, I noticed something remarkably peculiar: a soft kiwi that had managed to escape inspection. I decided to buy this daring rebel kiwi. My friend Jill, who stood next to me, exclaimed, "Oh, don't get that one; it's no good. Look at it; it's all soft!" I explained to her that I wanted this one because it was ripe. Inside the cafeteria I shared part of my kiwi with Jill, and she responded, "Hey, this is pretty good. Why is it so sweet though? Are kiwis supposed to taste this way?"

It helped that my parents talked to and listened to me on a regular basis. They asked me such questions as, "What happened today that made you feel the way you do?" Together, we discussed our daily discoveries. Simultaneously, my mother constantly shared with me the information she collected from the health books she was always busy reading.

Once, in third grade, we had pizza day, a celebration among all third graders that is usually marked on the calendar along with Christmas and New Year's Day. I was sitting with my friends, eating my fruit salad of apples, oranges, blueberries, raspberries, and honey, when a girl from a different class sat down next to me. I had learned from past experiences to anticipate trouble with her company.

"Look at this yummy pizza!" she said wobbling her wilting slice of pizza at me. "You can't have any, because you eat rabbit food!" she continued.

"I could have some if I wanted," I said, "but I just don't want to."

"Oh, really?" she mocked. "And why's that?"

"Well, if you must know," I said with a sigh, "it's because the bread was made out of genetically engineered wheat, which was sprayed with pesticides so toxic that the people working with it had to wear full-body suits and gas masks. The cheese on your pizza could be several years older than you, seeing as it is likely to have come from an expired army reserve. The tomatoes were picked green, placed in a refrigerator, and gassed red with ethylene. And the pepperoni might be made out of a number of hormone-laden animals, whose hygiene alone would be reason enough to abstain. Personally, I have no wish to eat such a combination. My parents knew the owner of a pizza restaurant, and he told them that his profits were through the roof, because each pizza cost him only pennies in ingredients."

The girls at my table stared at me in stunned silence, their slices of pizza frozen halfway to their mouths. I cheerfully continued eating my fruit salad. That night, my mother got a phone call from an angry lady demanding to know what I had told her daughter, who refused to eat her dinner.

It was these types of experiences that I needed to discuss with someone who understood my situation and could teach me to live more harmoniously among my peers. After countless conversations with my friends and family members, I now feel comfortable standing out. I have come to understand that, as illogical as it is, the majority is *not* always correct. Just because everyone else in the world is doing it doesn't mean it's the right thing to do. Sometimes the majority can be wrong. I have learned to think for myself, and this has helped me resist all kinds of social pressures. The key is to take an insult as you would a compliment. When people see that their comments do not bother me, they desist.

For example, a boy recently said to me, "Do you want some milk? Oh wait, I know you don't, because you are a monkey-woman. You eat granola. Ooo-oo-ah-ah-ah-AHa-oo!" Instead of responding with, "How dare you not support my eating choice, you chauvinistic imbecile, I thought you were my friend," I said, "Finally someone sees me for what truly I am. Where have you been all my life?" In my experience, fully accepting a negative comment is usually the best way to discharge it. This strategy leaves me feeling empowered and often makes for a good joke. If I take offense at the statement, all it means is that the insulting person is right and he or she has opened my eyes to an aspect of myself that needs some work.

People pressure others to do things only when they are insecure about their own choices. In most cases, when people have a problem, it has nothing to do with me, so I just allow those around me to feel and say whatever they do without taking it personally. I have no trouble dealing with peer pressure, because I understand that as long as I treat myself well, I will never be mistreated, regardless of how others respond to me. Doing what I have no wish to do, especially as an attempt to spare others discomfort, serves no one. It's important for me to eat foods that make me healthy, because I distinctly remember what it's like to be unhealthy. I understand what is true for me, and that is why it is no longer difficult for me to go to social events and interact with others. I feel that I can relate to anyone just by being human.

After the pizza incident, I decided to spruce up my school lunches a little. I started bringing exotic fruits to share, such as mangoes, pomegranates, papayas, pineapples, and even cherimoyas. I began preparing some raw foods that didn't look or taste "healthy." I began making my own fruit leathers (dried fruit rolls), which were a real hit among my friends. My brother was named "fruit boy" after bringing delicious fruits for lunch every day (which he never got to eat, because other kids usually ate them for him).

Despite the difficulties of helping children eat healthier, it is never impossible. Once, a woman and her five-year-old daughter, Jane, stayed with my family for three days. Jane refused to touch *any* raw food. She was so convinced that raw foods were awful that she simply would not try any. I decided to find one raw dish that she would like, so I made a smoothie out of one ripe mango, five strawberries, and one frozen banana. I poured the cool pink smoothie into a small, clear glass, placed a slice of orange on the side, and stuck a sprig of mint in the center. The glass quickly frosted over in tiny beads of water, which made it seem absolutely decadent. Jane watched me as I put this dish together. It looked mouthwatering on such a hot summer day.

"Oh yummy! This smoothie sure is good," I said, digging into it with an ice-cream spoon. "Are you sure you don't want any?"

"Yuck," Jane responded, "I hate raw food!"

"I don't know," I went on, "this tastes pretty good to me. Why don't you try just one spoonful? I won't be offended if it doesn't taste good to you. Who knows? It might not be so bad."

"There's no way I'm eating even one spoonful of that awful raw stuff!" Jane declared firmly.

I dropped the subject and finished the smoothie by myself. My neighbor Shannon stopped by, and I poured her a smoothie too. Emptying her glass, Shannon vocalized her delight at the flavor of this concoction. I wanted to make it clear to Jane that I was not about to force her to eat something she had no desire to eat, that I could respect her food choices and trust that she knew what was best for her. Asking her to try the smoothie was simply a suggestion that Jane had the right to ignore. However, it was important for me to get the message across that wholesome food could be delicious, so later that evening, I tried again.

"Jane, would you like to help me make some watermelon candy?" I asked.

"Yeah, okay," she said.

Together, we went to work in the kitchen. I peeled and sliced up a large watermelon, while Jane juiced three lemons. We dipped each slice of watermelon into the lemon juice and placed the slices onto trays in a dehydrator. When we were finished, we cleaned up the kitchen, and I thanked Jane for helping me.

The next morning, the kitchen was filled with a sweet aroma wafting from the direction of the dehydrator. Jane and I opened the dehydrator lid and peeked inside.

"Wow," said Jane, "The slices have become paper thin!" I peeled a slice of watermelon from the uppermost tray and took a bite out of it. "Is it good?" asked Jane.

"Yeah, it's really good," I said. "The watermelon seeds have become crunchy. Would you like to try a piece?"

Jane shook her head, no.

"How will you know what dried watermelon tastes like if you never try it?" I asked, breaking off a tiny piece the size of a button. "Here, eat this. If you don't like it, you can always spit it out."

Jane took the tiny piece of watermelon and popped it into her mouth. She didn't spit it out.

"It's pretty good, huh?" I said.

"Yeah," she responded, surprised, "it's not as disgusting as I thought it would be."

I just happened to mention that watermelon is a good source of vitamin A, which helps form and maintain healthy teeth, bones, and skin[16] and that it is also remarkably good for the eyes because it forms pigments in the retina that allow vision in dim light, which is helpful for people whose eyes are sensitive to sunlight.[17] Several hours later I found half of the dehydrator empty.

Later that day, Jane helped me cut corn off the cob for a salad, and I noticed her sneaking some corn into her mouth. When she realized that I had seen her do it, she grinned sheepishly. "So that's where all the corn has disappeared to!" I said.

By the time Jane and her mother left our house, Jane had no problem sampling raw foods and even found that she enjoyed many of them. She had come up with a few of her own tasty recipes and was excited about creating more of them. Before she left, this five-year-old girl gave my mother a very serious look and said, "Your daughter is very intelligent. You did a good job raising her!"

When feeding younger children a raw food diet, you can encounter the danger of attack from society. There were several occasions when my neighbors called social services to report my parents, claiming that they were not feeding my brother and me. On one such occasion, my brother and I were home alone when a stern-looking lady with a clipboard stopped by our house. When she knocked, we answered the door together. She introduced herself and asked us how old we were. We responded that Sergei was eleven and I was ten. She could see for herself that we looked well fed and definitely were not starving to death. "What did you have for lunch, Dear?" she asked my brother. Sergei sensed that this was an odd question for her to ask, because she did not seem like the type to be at all interested in health food. So, instead of explaining that we had eaten fresh, organic, raw foods for two years; that each of us had recovered from awful illnesses; and that we were working on perfecting a raw lasagna recipe, he decided to tell her this instead: "We just came back from McDonald's, where we each had a Big Mac with fries." This answer seemed to satisfy her, because she said, "Oh, okay then, Honey. You two have a nice evening." And then she left, never to be heard from again.

Sometimes, especially with older children, it might be necessary to simply let them eat what they want. I met a mother of four children, of whom two ate raw foods and two didn't. All of her children were over age twelve. She asked me what she should do, whether she should just make them all eat raw foods by entirely removing cooked foods from the house. I told her that I thought this was a bad idea because it would undoubtedly create stress and conflict in the family. She asked if she should continue buying them bread. I advised to not only continue buying them bread but also teach her children to make healthful cooked food, such as steamed veggies and porridge. There are more important things than health, such as love, happiness, and peace; eating poorly is not as harmful as living with feelings of resentment. I further explained that if she told her kids she accepted them totally regardless of what they ate but in reality did not, secretly wanting them to change, her face and voice would give her away, which would make matters even worse because then she would be lying. In an experiment where children who were forbidden to eat sweets, as well as kids who were not, were placed in a room filled with chocolates with no adults present, the children who had been restricted in their chocolate consumption ate dramatically more than those who had no such prohibition. In my own family, the relatives who were formerly resistant to eating more healthfully are now open to learning from us. Today, they freely call us up to ask for advice.

At times, my eating habits make other people uncomfortable. As much as I try to convince others that I really don't judge them for their eating habits and believe they have the right to eat whatever they want, often people still don't believe me. I realize that it is not my judgment they fear; it is their own. In the words of Byron Katie, "We freak out when we think others see us as we see ourselves."[18] Once, I was with some college friends who were eating Froot Loops and beer for lunch. One of them said to me, "Valya, you must be so disgusted by us." All I could find to say was, "No, I just love you guys." This conversation led me to shift my views even further. I used to say, "I love you for who you are, not what you eat." Afterward, I began to say, "I love you not only for who you are but also for what you eat! I love that you eat what you enjoy." This seems to be the most effectual method of debunking people's fears about my potentially judging them.

I believe there is little difference between children and adults. We are all participating in this moment for the first time, and although with age we begin to pretend to know what we are doing, we are still winging it most of the time. To quote Byron Katie again, "We often take the position of the teacher because we are afraid to be the student."[19] It is experience that children lack, not intelligence. There is nothing kids love more than to be spoken to as equals. They are so intelligent that it is often unnecessary to simplify things for them. I am frequently amazed at the depth of understanding children possess.

It is sad for me to see how often children are herded into different diets without any clue of the importance. When I speak to young people about health, I try to make very clear why I think it is so essential to be healthy. For me, health is a great blessing. I no longer have asthma to prevent my taking part in activities that add so much joy to my life, such as playing the flute, jogging, swimming, and other actions that focus on breathing. I am so grateful to my parents for teaching me to eat nutritiously. To be healthy means to live a life free of disease. It means remaining youthful throughout life, recovering quickly from accidents, and having plenty of energy with which to manifest our dreams. My dear friends, I wish you the best of luck in helping your children eat more healthfully.

TRaVELING WITH RaW FOODS

SERGEI: The persistently vast availability of unhealthful foods and scarcity of healthful options make it challenging to travel on a raw food diet. The third most common question I receive after "Where do you get your protein?" and "How do you interact with society?" is "How do you manage to travel while eating raw?" Many people seem to have difficulty sustaining themselves on raw foods while traveling. I would like to share some tips I have acquired while traveling around the world with my family.

There are two main challenges for raw foodists on the road. Challenge number one is finding good-quality raw produce wherever you go. This includes locating health food stores, produce stands, and even local farmers in or around your final destination. Challenge number two is coping with the cooked foods that surround you on your travels, such as the strong, sweet aromas that follow you on airplanes, buses, in hotels, and so forth. The good news is that you can kill two birds with one stone, so to speak. If you make food preparations ahead of time, your excursion will be "raw-food compliant," allowing you to go on and enjoy your trip relaxed and temptation free. Here is an example of what happened to my parents when they left for a trip unprepared.

Once, my parents flew to Puerto Rico from Texas. Prior to their departure they bought delicious, organic fruits and veggies to last them the duration of the flight and then some. However, U.S. customs took away all of their raw goodness before they boarded the flight. My parents had nothing left except water. Hungry upon arrival, they rushed to a supermarket but unfortunately found that every store in Puerto Rico had closed early due to a holiday. Left with no other options, my mom and dad rented a car and began the six-hour drive to the Ann Wigmore Institute. When they finally arrived at the institute at two o'clock in the morning, they were so hungry that they found someone's leftover energy soup in the refrigerator and gulped it down.

Instances like this are better off avoided, because they create unnecessary temptations. It can be very difficult for even the most hardcore raw foodists to stick to raw foods if they do not plan ahead. The one good thing about such situations is that they quickly teach us what *not* to do.

Before our family's next long trip, my parents made sure to plan ahead. They went to our local food co-op and bought some slightly overripe fruit in the discounted section. Then the four of us took this fruit, sliced it, and dried it in the dehydrator to be eaten as a sweet snack. Next, we bought some of our favorite vegetables—carrots, kale, celery, bell peppers, onions, mushrooms, cilantro, parsley, and tomatoes—and sliced them up into thin slices and dried them as well. Once dried, the veggies were mixed together in a bag to make rehydratable soup. You only need to add water, salt, and a little oil to taste, and you have a complete, delicious, organic raw meal! We also dehydrated several kinds of flax crackers and made some delicious dehydrated cookies. Finally, we mixed our own trail mixes with our favorite nuts, seeds, and raisins.

So this trip was a piece of (raw) cake! When mealtime came during our flight, we requested a bowl of warm water for each of us to rehydrate our dried soup. We made delicious sandwiches with our crackers and the vegetable slices served by the airline. When the aroma of our soup wafted over to the other passengers, they started to point at us and say, "We want what they're having!" For the rest of our trip we snacked on dried fruit and trail mix, which made traveling more exciting and less stressful. We enjoyed sharing our food with other people throughout our trip; our raw cookies were the most popular.

While one should always plan ahead, it is also important to remember why you are traveling in the first place! One of the things that stimulates me to travel is the exotic fruit! Maybe I will never get to try authentic Italian pizza or French cheese, but who cares when you compare pizza and cheese to the exquisite taste of tree-ripened jack fruit, or the decadent taste of a mangosteen! One of the many great benefits to eating raw is a heightened immune system so that you don't have to worry as much about getting sick from fruit. Of course, some caution is necessary, and it's a good idea to learn about new plants if you are unfamiliar with them, but as far as the chance of getting sick from fruit purchased from fruit stands, I have been to nine third-world countries without ever running into any problems. In fact, I always felt much better on my return! If I had never ventured far from home, I would never have encountered some of the most delicious fruits I've ever tasted. Enjoy your travels and plan ahead!

Benefits of Eating Green Leafy Vegetables

Green leafy vegetables are the most beneficial food for humans. Not only do they possess the vitamins and minerals that our bodies require for daily functions, but greens also present these nutrients in a way that is easily accessible to us. With all of the benefits that these miracle plants supply to humans, it's a wonder why I hesitated to incorporate more of them into my diet.

Nature is brilliantly designed to put the most precious answers right under our noses, to be discovered when the time is right. If we look at an abundant forest, we will notice that the vast majority of the plants filling it are green. Only a small percentage of the food found in a forest contains fruits. These fruits are often sparse, hard to harvest, and in season for a very short time. To me, this is a strong indication that humans needing to survive in nature could not rely on fruits alone! They would need to incorporate large amounts of greens to sustain themselves and remain healthy.

As I began introducing more of the color green into my diet, my energy levels began to skyrocket. The more I ate foods such as kale, chard, lettuce, and spinach and drank green smoothies (smoothies made from blending greens and fruits), the more I became interested in learning about this food category. In my search for the optimal food for humans, my attention was drawn to greens that grow in the wilderness. I started educating myself about wild edibles and found an incredible hidden gem.

While cultivated greens such as kale, lettuce, and collards offer immense nutrition to those who consume them, their nutritional value will never come close to that of wild greens. Greens found in nature have grown without human interference and therefore are hardier plants with longer roots. Their root systems can reach deep down into the mineral-rich forest soil and draw out trace minerals, which are unattainable through even commercially grown organic plants. Wild plants have not been hybridized and remain in their natural form, one that is undoubtedly more beneficial to humans. With all the benefits wild greens offer, knowing that this premium nutrition can be harnessed *for free* is the icing on the cake.

Have you ever wondered where people who don't consume animal products get their protein? Would you be surprised to learn that eating green leafy vegetables such as kale, collards, lettuce, spinach, and arugula provides your body with an adequate amount of protein that often surpasses the United States Department of Agriculture (USDA) recommended daily allowance? Would it shock you to discover that, apart from essential amino acids, greens also offer a plethora of other health benefits? In this section we will take a closer look at something that has taken me nearly fifteen years to realize: the true value of greens. My experience and studies have led me to conclude that green leafy vegetables are not only healthful for people to consume regularly but also essential for maintaining a healthy life. This section discusses three of the biggest benefits that come from choosing the color green: fiber, chlorophyll, and protein.

What Is Fiber and Why Do We Need It?

The main purpose of consuming fiber is elimination. Our bodies constantly struggle to filter the fuel we put into them. Just as an automobile fuel filter strains away unnecessary particles in gasoline that would otherwise eventually clog the car's engine, our bodies strain away useless matter to avoid clogging up. Because it would be dangerous to save and store various pollutants such as pesticides, chemicals, toxins, and dead cells, our bodies do everything in their power to eliminate what doesn't benefit them to ensure smooth running. Fiber plays an important role in this elimination process.

Under a microscope the fiber molecule resembles a sponge.[20] It is porous and absorbent, with the ability to soak up what the body does not need. By binding all the toxic matter into one package and sending it out through the bowels, the body manages to purify its system, remain healthy, and function properly without disease.[21]

My sister and I like to refer to fiber as the magic sponge. Have you ever tried to clean up a spill using something nonabsorbent? I have! I was once forced to clean up a large olive-oil spill without a sponge. I tried various methods, such as soaking up the oil with printing paper, squeezing the oil off the side of the counter into the compost, and even using my hand to try to pick up the grease. Nothing worked. In my futile attempts, I smeared oil everywhere and made a much bigger mess than the original spill. Finally, I realized I needed to abandon cleaning up until I had a sponge in hand.

Fiber is even better than a sponge, because it can absorb several times its own weight and volume. Without enough fiber, our bodies struggle to find a secondary method for eliminating waste and resort to drastic measures such as creating acne. Eliminating toxins through pimples takes a lot of effort and energy! Squeezing debris through our skin, which is made up of tiny holes, is about as efficient as taking out the garbage by cramming it through the holes of a screen door. Why not give your body, your most precious machine, a break and eat enough fiber?

How much fiber is enough? According to the USDA, each person should get 26–31 grams of fiber per day.[22] The average American consumes about half that daily requirement: 15 grams per day.[23] This is not surprising, considering that the standard American diet consists mainly of high-fat, low-fiber foods. On the other hand, one cup of collard greens contains almost 3.9 grams of fiber.[24] If you were to start your day with a smoothie made from four cups of collards (approximately one bunch) and seasonal fruit, you would meet your daily fiber requirement before your day even began.

In addition to promoting healthy elimination, fiber comes with many other perks:

· Balances pH level and maintains homeostasis

· Promotes weight loss

· Slows down sugar absorption

- Decreases chances of diabetes and improves previously diagnosed cases
- Prevents cancer
- Reduces cholesterol
- Keeps bowels working properly
- Prevents hemorrhoids and ulcers
- Strengthens the heart

Green leafy vegetables are an excellent source of fiber! Eating green salads, drinking green smoothies, and incorporating more greens into your recipes will guarantee an adequate fiber consumption, allowing you to reap all of these health benefits.

The Miracle of Chlorophyll

Chlorophyll is the green pigment in plants that harnesses the sun's energy through photosynthesis.[25] When you examine a piece of green kale, you see chlorophyll.

Chlorophyll is to plants what blood is to humans. When a plant produces energy from sunlight, it uses that energy to nourish itself by circulating vital vitamins and minerals through its veins. When you eat a leaf of Swiss chard or fresh parsley, you are receiving energy from the sun. The molecule of chlorophyll—which is very similar to human blood, differing only in the central atom—is easily absorbed by your body and serves numerous purposes. Your body uses chlorophyll for cleansing and healing its organs, battling pathogenic bacteria, and supplying oxygen wherever it is needed.[26] The darker the green leafy veggies, the more chlorophyll they contain and the more health benefits are locked inside of them.[27] Following are several more advantages of eating chlorophyll-rich food.

- Increases red blood cell count
- Prevents cancer
- Makes the body's pH level more alkaline

- Boosts immune system
- Improves vision
- Reduces inflammation
- Counteracts environmental toxins

Protein

Often, when asked whether or not I get enough protein from my diet, I become aware that the person inquiring is confused about what protein is. One common belief about this mysterious substance is that it is a part of a cow, pig, chicken, or fish. When you cut open an animal, your naked eye will see fat, muscle, bone, and protein, right? T. Colin Campbell, coauthor of the acclaimed book *The China Study*, writes: "There are hundreds of thousands of different kinds of proteins. These proteins are constructed as long chains of hundreds or thousands of amino acids, of which there are fifteen to twenty different kinds."[28]

These proteins are found in everything from beef to apples and are extremely important to consume. Of the fifteen to twenty different kinds of amino acids in existence, there are eight that our body cannot synthesize. These amino acids are known as essential amino acids and are what people refer to as protein. Because proteins wear out on a regular basis and must be replaced, we need to regularly receive these eight essential amino acids from our food to remain healthy and balanced.[29]

Then what is the best source of protein? Is it meat, beans, or soy products? One of the biggest misconceptions circulating around protein is the myth that all of our essential amino acids must come from one source. This is why many people look at animal products as the one and only viable protein source. This is a rather inaccurate outlook, because, while all of the essential amino acids may be present in meat loaf, they are not arranged in the correct order for humans. Our bodies have to pull each amino acid from the foreign chain and create a new one that fits our needs, which is a very cumbersome and stressful process. On the other hand, eating a baby-green salad presents these same essential amino acids to our bodies in an easily accessible manner. T. Colin Campbell writes, ". . . animal foods are considered to be high-quality proteins, while plant foods are low quality; the greatest efficiency does not equal greatest health. There is much compelling research indicating that plant proteins, which allow for slow and steady synthesis of new proteins, are the healthiest types of proteins."[30]

Green leafy vegetables contain the largest amount of protein of all plant foods. By eating a diet rich in greens, our bodies can continue performing such tasks as repairing tissues, building muscles and bones, and creating enzymes and hormones.[31] Thus, we can live healthy and happy lives! To find out more about the benefits of greens, I recommend reading *Green for Life* by Victoria Boutenko.

WILD EDIBLES: A True Superfood

When we are young, our parents educate us about our living environments. To educate children about nature and keep their toddlers safe, our guardians resort to labeling every berry, bug, blade of grass, and leaf as poisonous. It isn't long before a gentle forest seems like a plant-laden "death trap." While ultimately this type of early instruction about plants keeps children safer, I believe that it also contributes greatly to fears about the outdoors and begins to separate people from the natural world. As a result we become less sensitive to environmental issues such as deforestation, plant extinction, and climate change. After all, why should I care about plants when they are all trying to kill me? However, totally removing our children from the great outdoors has resulted in a new serious condition called *nature-deficit disorder.* In his book *Last Child in the Woods: Saving Our Children from Nature-Deficit Disorder,* researcher Richard Louv argues that kids are so plugged into television and video games, and so inexperienced with plants and animals that they've lost their connection to the natural world.[32]

In reality, the world of wild edibles is a joyous and gentle one that need not be feared, although caution is necessary when learning to identify edible from poisonous plants. Wild edibles contain miraculous healing properties that people have used for centuries until the era of our grandparents, just a few short generations ago. Whether you sip herbal teas, nibble wild berries on a hike, wild-craft greens for a smoothie, or simply decorate a salad with wildflowers, wild edibles come with an abundance of health-giving properties! Furthermore, the natural world was engineered to work in alignment with humans and animals, not against them. Through proper harvesting techniques, we can assist the plant community, helping it grow and prosper while it does the same for us! Janice J. Schofield, author of *Discovering Wild Plants: Alaska, Western Canada, the Northwest,* one of my favorite books about wild edibles, writes, "Selectively harvesting plant roots loosens soil, thus aerating the ground for the remaining roots, as well as for seeds that will germinate."[33]

A great mind once said, "A miracle is simply a change of perception." Thus, if we change our perception about nature, I am confident that we will see wild plants as our miracle! Personally, the more I learn about plants, the more I am amazed at how I could have feared them. To me, wild edibles are superfoods that should be praised and used whenever possible. For example, did you know that dandelion is rich in vitamins A, B, and C, as well as copper, phosphorous, potassium, iron, calcium, and magnesium? Did you know that dandelion lowers cholesterol, heals the liver, fights gout, lowers blood pressure, alkalizes the body's pH levels, and promotes emotional satisfaction? Were you aware that dandelion roots help prevent and fight diabetes and hypoglycemia?[34]

Knowing what you know now, how will you treat those wretched dandelion weeds that grow throughout your otherwise beautifully manicured lawn? Voila, with a mere change of perspective, the dandelion that was once a curse is now a miracle. Not to mention, dandelion makes a wonderful addition to green smoothies! Of course, make sure to pick dandelions only in places that are free of chemicals and pesticides.

In the summertime in Oregon, I run a company called Harmony Hikes, which leads people on scenic tours and wild-edible walks. I love my job, because I often get the pleasure of sharing with my customers what I have learned about edible wild plants, or as I like to call it, "the free supermarket." In the summer of 2007 I took an eighty-five-year-old lady on one of my wild-edible walks, and together we discovered that serviceberries, which her parents had always warned her were fatally poisonous, were in fact delicious and rich in vitamin C. Tears rolled down my friend's face as she carefully picked and ate the sweet, dark berries for the first time in her life.

The practice of safely identifying and harvesting plants from the forest is easy. Just as we have come to know what dandelions look like, we can learn to identify other wild plants. At some point during your life, you learned the difference between basil and dill or lettuce and tomatoes; in the same way, you can learn to distinguish stinging nettle from miner's lettuce.

I urge you to apply caution. There are approximately 150 relatively poisonous plants in North America. Be aware and learn to identify the following twenty-three most toxic plants:[35]

American yew	Mayapple
Atamasco lily	Ohio buckeye
Baneberry	Poison hemlock
Blue flag	Poison ivy
Buttercup	Poison oak
Butterfly weed	Pokeweed
Death camas	Southwestern coral bean
Dogbane	Star of Bethlehem
False hellebore	Water hemlock
Foxglove	Yellow flag
Horse nettle	Yellow sweet clover
Jimsonweed	

(List does not include poisonous mushrooms.)

While 150 plants may seem like a lot, keep in mind that there are thousands of plants in nature that can be safely eaten. To give you some perspective, Native Americans of North America used 1,882 different plants for food.[36] We can reap the benefits of great health from these plants. Many times, we don't even need to drive far to harvest delicious wild edibles, because tasty weeds often grow in our backyards, parks, prairies, and fields. My sister and I decided to simplify even further the process of collecting these gems, so we now grow weeds and wild greens in our garden. Now, instead of cucumbers and tomatoes, we plant lamb's-quarter, stinging nettle, purslane, and chicory.

At the end of this book, you will find a brief description of a few of the most common wild edibles native to North America. This information is enough to help you start incorporating more wild foods into your cuisine. For a more detailed list, please visit www.harmonyhikes.com. You may also look into wild-edible workshops in your area or purchase a book on wild edibles from your local bookstore. I have found these titles most helpful for wild edibles that grow on the North American West Coast: *Discovering Wild Plants: Alaska, Western Canada, the Northwest,* by Janice J. Schofield, and *Edible Wild Plants: A North American Field Guide,* by Thomas S. Elias and Peter A. Dykeman.

If you have not already encountered wild edibles, may this book be your introduction. To help you enjoy wild edibles, I have included some of my favorite wild-edible recipes. Enjoy!

THE ULTIMATE TIPS FOR RAW GOURMET COOKING

The switch in lifestyle from cooked to raw food can be awkward and scary. It is a change that requires us to completely reprogram our old habits. Initially, this is never an easy or fun experience. However, overcoming hardships leads to personal growth, increased satisfaction, a sense of accomplishment, and new skills. As in all new endeavors, practice and experience ease discomfort, allowing room for fun, play, and creativity. In this section, we will look specifically at how we have been conditioned to cook food and the differences involved in preparing raw meals. This will help you make sense of the raw-food kitchen, and assist in reprogramming the way you prepare food, without compromising flavors or appearance.

A Difference in Flavor

One difference between cooked food and raw is the presence of flavor. During the process of cooking, heat causes many tastes to evaporate and disappear. For example, when boiled, tomatoes lose their tanginess and become rather bland to the taste. This is why, when we cook, we become accustomed to having an abundance of different spices, to add flavor back to the food after it has evaporated.

Raw food does not involve cooking and therefore allows food to maintain its original flavors. Anyone who has ever eaten a ripe piece of fruit or tasted a freshly picked vegetable is aware of how tasty it is without alteration. These original tastes are so strong that they require little seasoning and are often ruined with over-flavoring. Newcomer chefs and experts alike often attempt to pack a recipe full of as many ingredients and spices as possible, because they think that more means better. This is a rather large misconception, because not only do the various flavors start competing and canceling out one another but also the complexity of the recipe itself becomes harder for the body to digest. The more I experiment with food, the more I realize that simplicity cannot be improved upon. All of the best things in life are simple.

This is why, when I have the choice to eat at either a raw-food restaurant or a salad bar, I often choose the salad bar. This does not imply that you should treat salad as a gourmet meal or that simple food cannot be exciting. It is possible to create light and delicious meals without compromising on exquisite appearance and flavor. The best way to accomplish a great-looking, amazing-tasting, and healthful meal is to taste your food! Isn't it simple? Whether you create your own recipe or use a recipe book, periodically taste what you are mixing, and adjust the flavor accordingly. Don't be afraid to change a recipe if you doubt its proportions. For example, if celery pâté calls for two teaspoons of salt, yet upon tasting it you notice that it is already salty from the naturally occurring sodium in the celery, add less salt. Do whatever you need to maintain the delicate taste. You can choose to skip salt altogether. Being a good chef requires three things: observation, creativity, and improvisation. If you are interested in learning more about adjusting flavors, it is discussed in greater depth later in this chapter, in the section titled "Understanding the Five Basic Flavors" (refer to page 44).

Raw Kitchen Tools

Every ordinary kitchen contains necessary tools for food preparation. A raw-food kitchen is no different. However, instead of a stove, pots, pans, eggbeaters, and oven mitts, a raw-food kitchen relies on a cutting board, a good set of knives, a blender, a food processor, and a dehydrator. When you're making cookies, using a food processor rather than preheating the oven can be rather awkward and take some getting used to. Likewise, learning how to use a knife so that it becomes an extension of your hand also takes some effort. Because we weren't taught by our mothers or at school the best way to use blenders and food processors, it's helpful to learn from the experts.

Being a visual learner, I constantly search for classes, courses, and people I can learn from. No matter whether it's a new technique for peeling garlic or blending a chocolate mousse, watching how a professional uses his or her tools helps me break my old habits and learn how to use my own tools better. An Internet search will help you find classes and workshops in raw-food preparation offered in many major cities around the United States. One valuable resource is the Living Light Culinary Arts Institute in Fort Bragg, California. Both my sister and I graduated from this school, which specializes in teaching how to prepare raw meals. You can contact them at www.rawfoodchef.com to learn about the assorted events they offer that cover all the bases.

One of my favorite ways to learn a new skill is through the Internet. By watching how-to videos on YouTube (http://www.youtube.com) or Google (www.google.com), I feel as though I am getting a private lesson in the comfort of my home—for free! If you have not already done so, try typing "how to make a green smoothie" into the search engine of one of these Web sites and see what comes up.

Time Management

Another aspect of raw food requiring some repatterning is the time that it takes to prepare food. As a whole, eating a raw food diet is quicker than cooking, because you never have to wait for an oven to cook your meal. It is easy and fast to whip up a pâté and throw together a salad. However, certain procedures, such as dehydrating and sprouting, require time. Have you ever followed a raw recipe that called for soaked nuts or seeds? If not, then you will in this book. If we have to soak nuts overnight, then how can we eat dinner now? How about raw bread? Making bread in the oven takes roughly a few hours, while dehydrating bread can take up to twenty-four hours. These kinds of procedures may seem incompatible with busy lives unless we realize that, unlike cooking, none of them requires constant care or attention. With a little advance planning, you can eat well and save time.

If you set bread in an oven and forget about it, you could very well burn to a crisp not only the bread but also your house. Dehydrators do not get as hot as ovens, and therefore do not require your constant attention. After placing bread in my dehydrator, I completely forget its existence and go about my day. Hours or days later, a pleasant aroma from the kitchen wafts into my nose, causing me to check my dehydrator and discover fresh bread to eat. I always make extra so that I do not have to engage in this process more than once a month. Learning how to manage raw food preparation gives you an advantage over everyone else in that you'll have more time to do whatever you want rather than spend time slaving away in the kitchen either making food or washing greasy dishes.

Sprouting nuts and seeds is another task that can be cumbersome unless you do it while you sleep. This is why many recipes suggest soaking nuts overnight. There's no sense in patiently waiting for almonds to sprout so that you can have a glass of almond milk, when you can do it in your sleep. Once or twice a week, I soak sesame seeds for milk. When brushing my teeth before bedtime, I pour water into a bowl and throw in a cup of seeds, which takes less than thirty seconds to do. When I awaken the next morning, I'm ready to blend my soaked sesame seeds for cereal without thinking how inconvenient it is to soak seeds!

Thus far, I have addressed three ways in which old cooking habits can clash with raw food preparation. By recognizing old patterns in ourselves, we take a major leap in the direction of change. Adjusting to new flavors, kitchen tools, and food preparation is not as intimidating as it seems. I suspect that the more you prepare raw food, the more it will become second nature so that one day, when you think back to the beginning, you'll laugh at how scary it once seemed.

UNDERSTANDING THE FIVE BASIC FLAVORS

To make delicious food, a raw food chef must be aware of the five basic flavors. There are five types of taste buds on your tongue. Each taste bud receives information about a different flavor. Some flavors taste bitter and some taste sweet, while others taste spicy. The five basic flavors the human tongue can taste are bitter, sweet, sour, salty, and spicy (one B and four S's).

The concept behind the five basic flavors is simple: the more flavors that you can fit into a dish, the more your taste buds will be stimulated. If all five flavors are used, your mouth will receive a maximum level of stimulation. We call this type of food "gourmet"! Have you ever wondered why a chef adds a pinch of salt to chocolate chip cookies or why bitter lemon zest is added to pie as a final touch? Now you know.

Obviously certain foods have one or more dominating flavors. For example, when making a sweet dessert, you refrain from oversalting it, because you are aware that the dominating flavor of cake is sweet. I am not aware of any recipe in which all five flavors dominate. Usually a dominating taste consists of no more than two flavors. A dominating taste is essentially a building block for a recipe. If you want to impress people with your food, you have to concentrate on creating a good foundation.

There is not one dominating flavor for every type of food. However, there are general guidelines. When making soup, you can choose to have sweet and sour flavors dominate for a sweet and sour soup, or spicy and salty flavors for chili. Regardless of which flavors you decide to build around, it is a good idea to identify, early on, which flavor you want to be most prevalent, and adjust the others accordingly.

All of this may seem intimidating at first, but it is rather easy. If you start with one flavor and begin gently adding others, your mouth will let you know which combinations it likes and does not like. I recommend tasting your food throughout preparation to guard against adding a flavor that disagrees with your palate. Always taste your food five times before serving it to others! Each time you taste it, ask yourself whether or not it is missing one of the five flavors. This will train your mouth to be your best critic. With practice you will know in the first taste whether your food is missing any ingredients. Here is a list of the five flavors with suggested foods and spices containing each flavor:

BITTER

aloe	cilantro	lettuce
arugula	cocoa nibs	mustard greens
bay leaf	cumin	parsley
bee pollen	curry powder	poultry seasoning
carob	dandelion greens	sage
cayenne pepper	dill	sesame seeds
celery tops	endive	

SWEET (DRIED OR FRESH)

agave nectar	mango	raisin
apple	melon	raspberry
apricot	mulberry	raw honey
banana	orange	stevia (fresh
bell pepper	papaya	or powdered)

cherry	peach	strawberry
date sugar	pear	tomato
date	persimmon	watermelon
fig	pineapple	
grape	prune	

SOUR

apple cider vinegar	lemon	rejuvelac
balsamic vinegar	lemongrass	rhubarb
blackberry	lime	sorrel
blueberry	nut or seed yogurt	sour cherry
cranberry	orange	strawberry
green apple	raspberry	tomato

SALTY

celery	sea salt (Celtic Sea Salt, Krystal Salt)
cilantro	sea vegetables (dulse, kelp, nori, arame,
parsley	kombu, hijiki)

SPICY

cayenne pepper	ginger	peppermint
chile pepper	habañero pepper	radish
cinnamon	horseradish	spearmint
clove	mustard greens	vanilla
garlic	nutmeg	wasabi
(greens and cloves)	onion (greens and bulb)	

It is important to note two more things pertaining to gourmet cooking. First, in its original state, raw food is rich in flavors, which should be recognized prior to making a recipe. Unlike cooked food, raw ingredients maintain many tastes, which have not been baked, boiled, broiled, or fried out. When incorporating the five flavors, these tastes should be taken into account to avoid disrupting the balance. Because apples are naturally sweet, it's unnecessary to add sweetener when making apple juice. Likewise, celery is naturally salty, so recipes calling for celery require much less salt. These natural flavors can also change depending on how the food was handled or grown. For example, when I make gazpacho, a cold tomato soup, I use a little sweetener to balance the flavors. However, when I purchase organic, ripe tomatoes from a farmers' market, I rarely add sweetener, because they bring their own sweet taste to the soup. If you get into the habit of tasting your ingredients before preparation as well as during, you will create nothing but bliss.

Secondly, not all recipes require using all five flavors. Juices, nut milks, smoothies, and simple foods can taste just as good, if not better, in their simple states. The principle of the five basic flavors is mostly relevant to gourmet dishes. A cool glass of hazelnut milk or juice from freshly picked strawberries tastes delectable without alteration. Adding too many flavors to such foods risks compromising their already delicious taste. You are welcome to add whatever flavors you want to try to stimulate your taste buds to the max. The law of the five basic flavors is not a law at all but merely an equation for making food taste good.

meet your new appliances

Sergei and Valya: With the surplus of different blenders, food processors, and dehydrators on the market today, it can seem impossible to make up your mind about which ones to purchase. Furthermore, with equipment prices ranging from fifteen to seven-hundred dollars, how can you be certain that choosing one brand over another ensures a quality product at a reasonable price? This section is dedicated to the equipment that makes up a successful raw food kitchen. We have tested all the appliances mentioned below over the course of fifteen years, in hundreds of food preparation demonstrations. Having literally created thousands of recipes using various machines, we managed to weed out each piece of equipment that was less than perfect until left with the absolute best! All of the items discussed below are tools that we use and recommend!

While having the following equipment will make your transition to a plant-based diet easier, more enjoyable, and less stressful, it is by no means essential. Like a new kitchen stove, a superior quality blender often comes with a high price tag, which is unrealistic for many people. If your household is low on money, save your money and rest assured that you can make do with whatever equipment you can get your hands on. For example, if you own a blender that is not as powerful as a Vita-Mix, that's okay! Simply blend your concoction longer, until it reaches a satisfying consistency. Ultimately the decision is yours, and whatever you decide is right!

Vita-Mix Blender $249–599

A blender is used for completely crushing up and liquifying ingredients to create dishes such as smoothies, soups, dressings, sauces, pie toppings, and puddings. Because many raw ingredients are rich in fiber and cellulose (a very tough plant matter), liquifying them often requires high levels of power and strength. We wholeheartedly recommend buying a Vita-Mix blender, because it meets our requirement for strength and power better than any other mixer on the market. While common blenders mix at roughly 11 miles per hour, the Vita-Mix rotates at 240 miles per hour.[37] Essentially, this means that if you dump some wooden blocks into a Vita-Mix container and add water, you will have a creamy log soup.

In a more practical application, the Vita-Mix blender allows the user to play around with consistency, resulting in everything from a chunky mixture (which is often preferred in soups) to a fluffy, creamy mixture (great for sweets, cake frosting, and puddings). Furthermore, the Vita-Mix can replace the need for a juicer when the liquified matter is strained through a strainer or nut-milk bag, separating the liquid from the solid.

If you place dried nuts, seeds, or grains into a Vita-Mix and blend them without water, the machine will pulverize these ingredients into flour. This is extremely handy for making garden burgers, pâté, hummus, and crackers. All around, the Vita-Mix is the most versatile piece of equipment, so if you can only afford one appliance, we advise you to start with the Vita-Mix blender.

Vita-Mix: www.vitamix.com, 1-800-848-2649

Alissa Cohen: www.alissacohen.com, 1-888-900-2529

Everything Kitchens: www.everythingkitchens.com,
1-866-852-4268

RawGuru: www.rawguru.com, 1-800-577-4729

Epinions: www.epinions.com, A convenient Web site for comparing kitchen appliances

Cuisinart Food Processor $100–200

Like a blender, a food processor grinds ingredients into smaller pieces. However, while a blender liquifies all ingredients, a food processor chops food into smaller pieces. With a wider holding container and S-shaped blades that don't extend to the edges of the container, the food processor becomes the perfect tool for making such foods as pâté, hummus, guacamole, pie crusts, and burgers. Food processors usually come with several handy additional blades, including a grater and a slicer, which are perfect for making specialty salads, chips, and marinated foods.

We recommend buying a Cuisinart. Not only are Cuisinarts strong and durable, but also their blades stay sharp longer than those of competitors, because they are made from quality metal. These blades easily grind through hard vegetables, nuts, seeds, and grains.

It is important to note that there are several different models available. We recommend the simple seven-cup model, because we find it to be the most efficient and user friendly. This model costs less and does not include a glut of puzzle pieces needing to be assembled in the right order for the machine to function properly.

CUISINART RESOURCES

Cuisinart: www.cuisinart.com, 1-800-726-0190

Everything Kitchens: www.everythingkitchens.com,
1-866-852-4268

Amazon.com: www.amazon.com

Epinions: www.epinions.com, a convenient Web site for comparing kitchen appliances

Excalibur Dehydrator $109–250

A dehydrator can be considered the oven of the raw food kitchen, except instead of using extreme heat to process food, a dehydrator, or dryer, blows warm air (usually around body temperature, ninety-eight degrees) over food in a contained environment. This process draws water out of food, thereby preserving it and concentrating its flavor.

Food dryers are essential for making such snacks as chips, crackers, breads, cookies, and travel foods. If you like dried fruit or happen to obtain an abundance of overripe produce, you can create delicious, nutrient-rich snacks by dehydrating them.

Of all the dehydrators we have tested, our favorite is the Excalibur. Not only is it reasonably priced for a commercial dehydrator, but also it is made with exceptional craftsmanship and ingenuity. Unlike its competition, the Excalibur was built with the heating fan placed vertically and at the back of the unit. This ensures that every tray receives an even amount of heat, regardless of whether it is located at the top, middle, or bottom. The end product is a well-rounded, consistent, tasty food.

One of the best advancements of the Excalibur is that its temperature can be adjusted by a dial located on top of the unit. While the basic rule of thumb is to try to dry everything as close to body temperature as possible, one should be aware of several exceptions. For example, when drying moisture-rich foods such as melons and tomatoes, cranking the heat up to 112–115 degrees for the first six hours prevents these foods from getting moldy. The presence of moisture in the food keeps the temperature inside it lower than that of the air in the dehydrator.

Finally, it is important to note that the Excalibur has several different models on the market. We recommend the nine-tray model 2900. There are smaller, cheaper models; however, they all draw approximately the same amount of electricity as this one without a substantial price break. With the nine-tray model, you can make food in a large batch, preventing the need to make a mess in your kitchen every other day. Even if you live alone, in the long run, having nine trays is much more practical.

EXCALIBUR DEHYDRATOR RESOURCES
Excalibur: www.excaliburdehydrator.com, 1-800-875-4254
Canning Pantry: www.canningpantry.com, 1-800-285-9044
Kitchen Universe: www.kitchen-universe.com,
1-800-481-6679
Become: www.become.com, another convenient Web site for comparing kitchen appliances

Champion Juicer $180–259

A juicer extracts liquids from fruits and vegetables, and separates the pulp. Generally juicers are not considered versatile machines, because most are engineered for the sole task of extracting juice. This is starting to change as more and more companies develop ways of implementing juicers for various other tasks.

The Champion juicer is our favorite, because it includes several attachments that allow you to make ice cream, nut butters, and pâtés in addition to juices. Juicers tend to be complicated, with lots of little pieces needing to be assembled prior to using them, but the Champion juicer has a total of five pieces, which are easy to assemble and clean.

CHAMPION JUICER RESOURCES
Champion Juicer: www.championjuicer.com, 1-866-935-8423
On the World Wide Web: www.discountjuicers.com
HealthWisdom: www.healthwisdom.com, 1-888-337-8646
Rhio's Raw Energy: www.rawfoodinfo.com, 1-212-941-5857

Spiralizer $25–100

A spiralizer is used to shred vegetables and hard fruits into noodle form. This tool makes it easy to create dishes such as lasagna, pasta, and macaroni. Unlike a regular grater, a veggie spiralizer has different blades that help process food into beautiful, symmetrical shapes and sizes. Furthermore, spiralizers have a built-in mechanism that prevents veggies from ripping, ensuring a long and continuous noodle strand. Of the numerous spiralizer models available, we have used many different ones and liked them all.

VEGGIE SPIRALIZER RESOURCES

Livingnutrition: www.livingnutrition.com, 1-707-566-0404

Raw Life: www.rawlife.com, 1-866-Raw-Paul (729-7285)

Target: www.target.com

NaturalZing: www.naturalzing.com, 1-301-703-4116

Nut-Milk Bag $8–12

Nut-milk bags are used to strain liquid away from the fibrous, pulpy material. A nut-milk bag is a wonderful tool that each household should have on hand. This simple device can ease the process of making nut and seed milks, juices, pâtés, cookies, and sprouts. There are many online sources that sell nut-milk bags; however, it is extremely easy to make one, so it's a good idea to consider this option before buying.

To make a nut-milk bag, you need to obtain some sort of mesh or loose-knit natural fiber and a drawstring, and have access to a sewing machine. By folding the mesh into a square, sewing around the edges, and adding a drawstring to the top, you can create a cheap and efficient nut-milk bag and begin straining away!

NUT-MILK BAG RESOURCES

Raw Family: www.rawfamily.com, 1-541-488-8865

Alissa Cohen: www.alissacohen.com, 1-888-900-2529

The Raw Gourmet: www.rawgourmet.com, 1-888-316-4611

1-877-My-Juicer.com: www.877myjuicer.com, 1-877-My-Juicer (695-8427)

Cutting Board $1–40

A cutting board does not require much explanation; it is a board for cutting food! Since raw food requires quite a lot of cutting, we recommend finding a cutting board that works for you and your living situation. This may be a thick wooden cutting board or a thin, malleable one. There is no right or wrong, so choose freely. The bottom line is that you and the board will develop a relationship in the coming years. To help you follow through on your commitment to raw foods, you may want to find a board that you love from the very beginning!

CUTTING BOARD RESOURCES

Amazon.com: www.amazon.com

Ross Dress for Less: rossstores.com, carries a variety of high-quality, low-priced cutting boards.

Chef's Resource: www.chefsresource.com, 1-866-765-Chef (2433)

The Cutting Board Company: www.cuttingboardcompany.com, 1-866-247-2409

Knives $2–200

As mentioned previously, raw food requires massive amounts of cutting. Find a knife or set of knives that you like and keep them in a convenient place. The price of a set of knives does not indicate good quality or whether you will like them. We have used hundreds of knives in various price ranges and have come to the conclusion that buying cheap knives is a waste of money, because they get dull fast, leech unhealthy materials into food, and can be potentially dangerous to work with!

On the other hand, purchasing knives in the three-figure range buys unnecessary worry that something might happen to them. The best knives that have graced our hands have always been within the fifteen-to-twenty-dollar range. They are sharp, and have a comfortable handle and a reasonable weight (not too heavy or light), which is what we look for when knife shopping!

Amazon.com: www.amazon.com

Target: www.target.com

Grater $4–12

A grater, which is used to shred vegetables and hard fruit, is a useful tool to have! Not only do we use our grater daily when adding color and texture to our salads but also when decorating gourmet food. One thing to keep an eye out for when buying a grater is an attachable container. Some graters come with a container that catches the shredded food particles, which is extremely useful because it reduces mess and prevents color mixing.

GRATER RESOURCES

Amazon.com: www.amazon.com

Target: www.target.com

TWO

Savory Dishes

APPETIZErs anD FInGer FOODS

An appetizer is a food or drink that stimulates the appetite before a meal. An appetizer, or "appetite teaser," is served to accentuate hunger and the overall desire for food. Appetizers are generally small in individual size and quantity, because they are meant to stimulate the taste buds, not fill the stomach. Just about any recipe can be served as an hors d'oeuvre by simply presenting it in miniature. For example, a simple marinated kale salad may not seem that exciting when served in an old bottomless bowl; however, if served on a tiny dish garnished with fresh herbs and cherry tomatoes, and sprinkled with drops of olive oil and balsamic vinegar, the same salad inspires mouth watering at the mere thought of indulging in this savory concoction. In this section we present numerous appetizers that have been very successful in our teachings and caterings. We encourage you to follow these recipes and see how you like them. Moreover, we hope that you will be inspired to alter and add to them, creating your own original appetizer recipes that woo many mouths to salivate.

TINY PIZZAS

CRUST

2 large zucchinis
2 cups soaked sunflower seeds
½ bunch oregano
½ teaspoon salt

Shape into flat patties on a dehydrator tray. Dry for 12 hours.

AMAZING TOMATO SAUCE

1 cup dried tomatoes, soaked 15 minutes
1 bunch cilantro
⅓ bunch basil
½ cup water
½ lemon juiced
1 clove garlic
4 tablespoons olive oil
½ teaspoon salt

Blend thoroughly.

CHEESE

½ cup nutritional yeast
¼ cup lemon juice
4 tablespoons agave nectar
¼ teaspoon poultry seasoning
¼ teaspoon salt

Mix thoroughly and pour onto dehydrator tray. Dry for 12 hours. Spread the Amazing Tomato Sauce onto the crust. Slice the cheese into slices and sprinkle on top. Garnish with olives. Serves 10.

FRESH SALAD ROLLS

1	pint cherry tomatoes, chopped in half
½	bunch green onions, diced
3	sprigs thyme, chopped
½	cup cashews, chopped
1	tablespoon olive oil
½	teaspoon sea salt
1	sprinkle black pepper

Mix all ingredients together. Tightly wrap desired amount of salad in romaine lettuce. Garnish with seasonal fruits and veggies. Drizzle with lime juice and serve. Yields 4–6 rolls.

COLLARD ROLLS

1	cup arame seaweed, soaked in warm water 15 minutes
3–4	cloves garlic, minced
2	tablespoons sesame seeds
1	red bell pepper, diced
1	strawberry papaya, peeled, seeded, and chopped
1	tablespoon olive oil
½	teaspoon sea salt

Mix all ingredients in a bowl and let stand for up to 30 minutes, allowing the seaweed to absorb the flavor of the other foods. Prepare collard greens by cutting the stems away from the leaves. Roll desired amount of salad into green leaves. Slice into small rolls or eat as is. Garnish with sunflower sprouts before serving. Yields 4–6 rolls.

ENDIVE TOWERS

1   cup pine nuts
2–3   cloves garlic
½   bunch cilantro
½   lime, juiced
¼   teaspoon sea salt

Blend all ingredients in food processor in short bursts. The object
is to mix the ingredients together without pulverizing them. Using
white or red endive, begin filling leaves with small amounts of pâté.
Place individually stuffed leaves of endive on top of each other,
perpendicular to the previous one. Stack endive 5 to 6 leaves tall.
Garnish with fresh herbs, sprouts, veggies, and fruits. Serves 3–4.

TOMATO-BASIL CITRUS SALAD

1   medium grapefruit, peeled, seeded, and
        chopped
3–4   medium-ripe tomatoes (preferably from a
        farmers' market), sliced thin
½   bunch fresh basil, chopped
1   tablespoon olive oil
1   tablespoon balsamic vinegar
¼   teaspoon sea salt

Be sure to peel the inner skin off the grapefruit. Mix all ingredients
thoroughly in a bowl. Chop additional amount of basil and spread
over top of clean plate. With an ice-cream scoop, scoop out
one serving of salad and place atop basil on plate. Garnish with
seasonal fruits and veggies. Repeat process for each additional
plate. Yields 4–5 scoops of salad.

TROPICAL SCOOP

1	strawberry papaya, peeled, seeded, and chopped
1	pint strawberries, chopped
2	golden kiwis, peeled and chopped
1	banana, chopped
1	pear, peeled, seeded, and chopped
¼	teaspoon powdered cloves
¼	teaspoon powdered nutmeg
1	teaspoon agave nectar
1	young coconut (meat and water)
4	dates, pitted
½	teaspoon vanilla

Mix first 8 ingredients thoroughly in a bowl. Blend young coconut, dates, and vanilla in a blender. With an ice cream scoop, scoop out one serving of salad and place atop clean plate. Using a spoon or squeeze bottle, pour a small amount of coconut cream atop the fruit mound. Garnish with seasonal fruits and mint. Repeat process as many times as necessary. Yields 4–5 scoops of salad.

salaDs

Salads are a crucial part of any raw-food enthusiast's diet. In the words of actor Woody Harrelson, "If you want to be successful at being raw, then you have to learn how to make really good salads!"[1] While creating a salad may seem easy, a diet that leads one to eat numerous salads on any given day can soon become boring from lack of variety. So, the challenging part is not whether you can make a tasty salad but whether you can make enough delicious salads to keep you excited day after day. Luckily, there is enough variety in produce to make this possible. We encourage you to visit your local supermarket, health food store, or farmers' market to get acquainted with the raw fruits and veggies with which you are unfamiliar. Doing so will significantly increase the amount of diversity, creativity, and taste that you experience in your day-to-day life. In this section we have compiled some of our all-time best salads for you to try. Enjoy!

CUCUMBER YAM SALAD

1	large yam, grated
5	small pickling cucumbers, sliced
2	tablespoons coconut oil
½	lemon, juiced
½	teaspoon sea salt
2	tablespoons nutritional yeast

Mix ingredients in a bowl and serve. Note: this salad is tasty in wraps made with collard greens. Serves 2–3.

VALYA'S FAVORITE SALAD

½	head white cabbage, thinly sliced
½	avocado, sliced long and thin
¼	white onion, diced
¼	cup fresh dill, chopped
2	tablespoons grape seed oil
½	lemon, juiced
¼	cup dulse leaf, chopped into small squares

Mix ingredients in your favorite bowl and enjoy. Serves 1–2.

SEAWEED TAHINI SALAD

½	head red leaf lettuce, chopped
1	medium tomato, sliced long and thin
½	avocado, sliced long and thin
½	arame sea vegetable, soaked 3 minutes in warm water, then strained
1	tablespoon raw tahini

1	teaspoon lemon juice
1	tablespoon Nama Shoyu
1	tablespoon olive oil
1	teaspoon honey or agave sweetener
1	teaspoon sea salt

Blend tahini, lemon juice, Nama Shoyu, olive oil, honey, and sea salt in the blender to a creamy consistency. Pour dressing over chopped ingredients and mix thoroughly. Serves 1–2.

CAULIFLOWER SALAD

½	head cauliflower
2	tablespoons olive oil
1	tablespoon lemon juice
½	bunch green onions
¼	cup cilantro, chopped
½	teaspoon sea salt
1	teaspoon onion powder

Chop veggies and toss in a bowl to mix with the rest of the ingredients. Then, grab a buddy and enjoy. Serves 1–2.

BEET SIDE SALAD IN A GLASS

3	beets, peeled and cubed
5	garlic cloves
1	teaspoon lemon juice
1	tablespoon olive oil
1	teaspoon honey
1	teaspoon sea salt
1	generous pinch fresh oregano, chopped

Blend first six ingredients in food processor. Garnish with oregano. Serves 2–3.

I CAN'T BELIEVE IT'S JUST CABBAGE

½   head white cabbage, thinly sliced
1   tablespoon olive oil
1   tablespoon lemon juice
⅓   teaspoon sea salt
1   tablespoon nutritional yeast

Mix all ingredients in a bowl and garnish with herbs or julienne-cut carrots. Serves 2–3. See plate 5.

SPICY TOMATO SALAD

5   Roma tomatoes, sliced long and thin
½   bunch fresh dill, chopped
1   tablespoon olive oil
¼   red onion, chopped in thin slices
½   teaspoon sea salt

Mix in a bowl and serve. Serves 2–3. See plate 4.

RUSSIAN CARROT SALAD

7   carrots, grated
4   cloves garlic
¼   cup fresh parsley, chopped
1½ tablespoons olive oil
½   teaspoon salt
1   teaspoon honey
¼   cup raisins
1   tablespoon nutritional yeast (optional, but offers scrumptious taste that will leave you wanting more)

Mix all ingredients in a bowl and devour! Serves 2–3.

CUCUMBER THAI SALAD

If prepared carefully, this elegant salad is sure to woo any crowd, whether or not they are raw foods enthusiasts.

4	small cucumbers, sliced into thin rounds
½	lemon, juiced
¼	cup cilantro, chopped
½	cup red onion, diced
1	teaspoon hot curry powder
1	teaspoon turmeric powder
½	teaspoon sea salt
1	teaspoon honey
¼	cup cashew pieces, crushed
½	tablespoons olive oil

Combine ingredients in a bowl. For consistent flavor throughout the dish, make sure the honey is mixed completely. Garnish with a sprig of cilantro. Serves 2–3.

COLORFUL FALL SALAD

3	cups sweet corn, cut from cob (or 1 10-ounce bag frozen corn, defrosted)
3	large Jerusalem artichokes, diced
1	Roma tomato, diced
2	green onions, diced
1	tablespoon Nama Shoyu
1	tablespoon balsamic vinegar
1–1½	tablespoon olive oil
¼–½	habañero pepper, minced

Mix all ingredients in a bowl and enjoy! Serves 2–3.

ONION SALAD

1½ red or white onions, chopped
¼   cup fresh basil or dill, chopped
2   tablespoons olive oil
½   lemon, juiced
½   teaspoon sea salt

Mix all ingredients in a bowl and serve with your favorite raw-food entrée. Serves 4–5.

CRANBERRY-ALMOND CARROT SALAD

8   carrots, grated
½   cup fresh basil, coarsely chopped
2   tablespoons olive oil
¼   cup dried cranberries
¼   almonds, crushed
½   lemon, juiced
½   teaspoon sea salt

Mix all ingredients in a bowl. Wait 15 minutes before serving to allow time for the flavor of the cranberries to seep throughout the dish. Serves 3–4.

MARINATED KALE SALAD

1   bunch green or purple kale
3   tablespoons olive oil
3   tablespoons balsamic vinegar
½–1 teaspoon sea salt

1½ tablespoons agave nectar or honey
½ orange, juiced
3–4 radishes, thinly sliced
½ red, yellow, or orange bell pepper
¼ cup pine nuts or hemp seeds

Rip the kale off its stalks into a bowl, reserving the stalks to make a green smoothie later on. In a blender, blend the olive oil, vinegar, salt, agave, and orange juice. Pour the liquid over the kale and mix thoroughly. It helps to use your hands to mix and squeeze the juices into the kale. Chop the remaining ingredients and add to kale. Serve on an elegant plate garnished with fresh herbs. Serves 1–2. See plate 5.

CHIMP SALAD (NO DRESSING REQUIRED)

This salad was inspired by our mother's research on the diet of chimpanzees, which consists predominately of fruits and green leafy vegetables. Sergei created this salad when living in Hawaii without a blender, which is why it requires no dressing.

1 ripe papaya
1 ripe banana
½ Fuji apple
1 ripe, juicy pear
1 sweet tangerine
½ avocado
¼–½ pound fresh organic baby-green salad mix
½ lime, juiced

For volume and texture, chop each piece of fruit into different sizes. Mix with baby greens, drizzle lime juice over the salad, and eat! Serves 2–3.

TOMATO SALAD

5	large tomatoes, chopped
1	large avocado, chopped
¼	bunch celery, chopped
2	tablespoons safflower oil
½	teaspoon sea salt
¼	cup dulse flakes, finely chopped

Mix in bowl and enjoy! Serves 3–4.

ASIAN SALAD

1	bunch baby bok choy
1	bunch collard greens
¼	cup olive oil
¼	cup Nama Shoyu
1	pinkie-sized piece of ginger, chopped
4	cloves garlic
¼	cup agave nectar
¼	apple juice or cider

Coarsely chop greens and mix in a bowl. Blend the remaining
ingredients in a blender until smooth and creamy. Combine with
greens. Wait 15 to 20 minutes before serving. Serves 2–3.

FENNEL ROOTS

1	small rutabaga
1	small turnip
½	celery root (celeriac)
1	small daikon radish
1	pinkie-sized piece of ginger, diced
¼	cup fresh fennel, diced

2   tablespoons olive oil
½   orange, juiced
½–1 teaspoon sea salt

Grate all root veggies. Mix with fennel and liquids. Serve on a colorful plate. Serves 2–3.

CASEY BOURGEOIS SALAD (BUTTERY PEAS)

10   ounces frozen peas, defrosted in warm water
2   tablespoons olive or coconut oil
1   tablespoon nutritional yeast
1   tablespoon balsamic vinegar
½   teaspoon sea salt

Mix all ingredients in a bowl and enjoy! Serves 2–3.

MICROGREEN SALAD

¼   pound baby green, or mesclun, mix
2   carrots, grated
¼   cup microarugula greens
¼   cucumber, sliced in rounds
1   tomato, chopped
1   tablespoon olive oil
1   tablespoon balsamic vinegar
1   tablespoon nutritional yeast
¼   teaspoon sea salt

Mix all ingredients in your favorite bowl and enjoy. Serves 1–2. See plate 3.

SIMPLE BUT DELICIOUS SALAD

1	bunch romaine lettuce, torn
2	Clementine tangerines, peeled and split into individual slices
½	cucumber, sliced into thin rounds
½	avocado, sliced into long, thin slices
½	Meyer lemon, juiced

Toss first four ingredients on an elegant plate. Drizzle lemon juice over the salad. Serves 2.

MIXED BEAN SALAD

2	cups green lentils
1	cup garbanzo beans
2	garlic cloves, minced
2	green onions, chopped
1	tablespoon coconut oil
½	teaspoon cumin powder
½	teaspoon beet powder
¼–½	teaspoon sea salt

Soak lentils and garbanzo beans overnight in lukewarm water. Drain and rinse beans. Transfer into a bowl and mix with other ingredients. Serves 2–3.

SAVOY CABBAGE SALAD

1	medium head Savoy cabbage, chopped into 1-inch-thick squares
1	Fuji apple, peeled and sliced long and thin
1	handful raw cashew pieces

Great with Savoy Dream Dressing (page 71).

RUSSIAN CUCUMBER SALAD

2   medium cucumbers, sliced into rounds
2   medium tomatoes, sliced
¼   bunch parsley, chopped
2   cloves garlic, minced
1   tablespoon safflower oil
¼   teaspoon sea salt

Mix all ingredients together in a bowl. Serves 1–2.

ROSEMARY ENDIVE SALAD

2   heads green endive, sliced
2   heads purple endive, sliced
¼   cup kumquats, sliced into thin rounds
5   sprigs rosemary, chopped
¼   cup cherry tomatoes
2   tablespoons olive oil
1   teaspoon sea salt

Mix all ingredients in a bowl. Garnish and enjoy! Serves 2.

BARLEY SALAD

2   cups barley, soaked overnight
¼   bunch dill
½   cucumber, chopped
1   red bell pepper, chopped
¼   red onion
¼   teaspoon salt
2   tablespoons agave nectar
3   tablespoons olive oil

Mix all ingredients in a bowl. Garnish and enjoy. Serves 3. See
photo of Barley Salad Yam Wrap, plate 2.

ROMAINE POMEGRANATE SALAD

1   head romaine lettuce, chopped or torn
1   medium avocado, sliced into long, thin strips
1   medium cucumber, chopped
1   pomegranate, peeled and seeded (only the
     seeds will be used)
¼   cup pine nuts
1   tablespoon olive oil
1   teaspoon agave nectar
½   teaspoon sea salt

Mix all ingredients in bowl and serve. Note: pomegranate increases red blood cell count. Serves 3.

GREEN CITRUS SALAD

1   head romaine lettuce, chopped or torn
3–4 Clementine tangerines, peeled and sliced
1   large cucumber, peeled and sliced into rounds
1   medium avocado, thinly sliced
¼   lime, juiced

Mix all ingredients in a bowl. Garnish with your favorite herb, such as thyme, rosemary, or mint. Top with lime juice, or drizzle with olive oil and lightly salt. Serves 3.

NOVEMBER SALAD

1   head romaine lettuce, chopped or torn
2   carrots, peeled and grated
¼   cup fresh cranberries
¼   cup fresh blueberries
1   medium avocado, sliced thinly
¼   cup sunflower sprouts

1   pinch basil leaves
1   pinch dulse leaves

Mix all ingredients in a bowl and dress. Great with Tahini Garlic
Dressing (page 73).

Dressings

Just as salads are essential to a raw-food diet, yummy dressings may
be equally important, because they provide a gourmet taste, even
to the simplest salads. For example, green leafy veggies, a prime
source of nutrition for raw foodists, can be a struggle to consume
because of their strong chlorophyll flavor. However, with a scrumptious dressing on hand, the strong taste of green will recede, making it easy to enjoy eating everything from lettuce to collards. Also,
knowing how to make a delectable sauce gives you the freedom to
dine out with companions who don't share your exact food interests. Most ordinary restaurants have a salad menu but don't offer
healthful dressings. Instead of ordering Thousand Island, we prefer
to bring our own freshly made organic dressing. This not only improves the quality of our food but also helps avoid having to explain
or justify the raw food lifestyle.

SAVOY DREAM DRESSING

¼   cup cashews
2   tablespoons lemon juice
2   tablespoons water
1   tablespoon olive oil
1   tablespoon agave nectar
½   teaspoon sea salt

Blend dressing in a blender for 2 minutes or until smooth. Mix
dressing with salad and serve. Serves 1–2. Great with Savoy
Cabbage Salad (page 68).

SUMMER BASIL DRESSING

1	large tomato
½	bunch basil
1	cup distilled water
½	avocado
¼	cup balsamic vinegar
¼	cup olive oil
1	tablespoon raw honey
1	teaspoon sea salt

Blend all ingredients in a blender for 3 minutes or until smooth. Serves 4.

BLACKBERRY DRESSING

1	cup fresh blackberries
1	cup distilled water
¼	avocado
¼	cup olive oil
¼	cup lemon juice
1	teaspoon sea salt
1	tablespoon raw honey

Blend all ingredients in a blender for 3 minutes or until smooth. Serves 4.

YUM DRESSING

½	cup lemon juice
¼	cup nutritional yeast
½	teaspoon poultry seasoning
¼	teaspoon sea salt
2	tablespoons agave nectar

Blend in a blender until smooth. Pour over your favorite salad and enjoy! Serves 3.

TAHINI DILL DRESSING

1 tablespoon tahini (sesame seed paste)
¼ bunch fresh dill
½ lime, juiced
1 teaspoon raw agave nectar
½ teaspoon sea salt
½ cup water

Pulse in blender until tahini is mostly mixed but dill is not pulverized. Serves 2–3.

TAHINI GARLIC DRESSING

2 tablespoons tahini
¼ cup apple juice
1 clove garlic
1 tablespoon olive oil
½ teaspoon sea salt

Blend all ingredients in a blender until smooth. Serves 3.

RAW KETCHUP

½ cup dried tomatoes, soaked in water 15 minutes
1 tablespoon apple cider vinegar
1 tablespoon raw agave nectar
1 tablespoon onion powder
½ teaspoon sea salt

Blend all ingredients in a blender until smooth. Use ketchup to season a burger or serve with veggies and herbs. Serves 3–4. See plate 11.

SWEET AND SOUR

1 cup water
½ bunch basil
1 tablespoon honey
1 large tomato
2–3 cloves garlic
1 tablespoon honey
½ teaspoon salt
½ lemon, juiced

Blend all ingredients in a blender until smooth. Serves 3–4.

SIMPLE TAHINI DRESSING

1 cup water
¼ cup olive oil
¼ cup lemon juice
1 tablespoon raw tahini
2 cloves garlic
½ teaspoon salt

Blend well in a blender. Serves 3.

LIGHT TOMATO DRESSING

2 large ripe tomatoes
3 stalks celery
  chile pepper to taste
1 tablespoon olive oil
1 tablespoon apple cider vinegar
1 teaspoon sea salt
2 tablespoons honey

Blend all ingredients in a blender until smooth. Serves 3–4.

PECAN DRESSING

½	cup pecans
½	bunch fresh oregano
4	stalks rhubarb
1	tablespoon honey
1	small jalapeño pepper
1	tablespoon olive oil
1	teaspoon salt

Blend all ingredients until smooth. Serves 3–4.

CREAMY TOMATO DRESSING

¼	cup olive oil
2	large tomatoes
½	teaspoon sea salt
½	cup almonds
1	tablespoon honey
¼	cup lemon juice
½	bunch celery or parsley

Blend all ingredients until smooth. Serves 4.

GRAVY

2	cups pecans, soaked
1½	cups water
½	cup dehydrated onion
1	tablespoon poultry seasoning
2	tablespoons olive oil
	salt to taste

Blend all ingredients thoroughly, to the consistency of gravy.
Serves 5–6.

COCO-YUM

1	young coconut (only the meat will be used)
2	tablespoons olive oil
3	stalks celery
½	cup water
½	medium-hot pepper
¼	cup lemon juice
1	tablespoon honey
½	teaspoon salt

Blend all ingredients thoroughly in a blender. Serves 5.

THAI SAUCE

¼	cup lemon juice
¼	cup Nama Shoyu
3	cloves garlic
¼	cup chopped ginger
1	tablespoon honey

Blend all ingredients until smooth and creamy. Note: this is a great dressing for Asian cuisine, such as nori rolls or noodles. Serves 6.

SOUPS

Soups were a type of food we never expected to eat again after switching to raw foods. With a little hard work and some creative brainstorming, we have created many delicious soups, proving that one should never say never. With new advancements in blender technology, it is even possible for raw foodies to eat warm soups. By simply blending any given soup recipe for a minute longer in the blender, the soup heats up from blade friction, adding that last bit of comfort on a cold winter morning!

GREEN-O-LICIOUS SOUP

1   avocado
1   bunch basil
1   orange bell pepper
1   cucumber
1   lemon (seeds removed to avoid bitterness)
2   cups fresh spinach
⅓   teaspoon salt (optional)
5   small white mushrooms, sliced
½   avocado, cubed
2   cups fresh spinach, chopped
2   stalks celery, chopped
1   additional cucumber, chopped

Blend first 7 ingredients thoroughly and pour into a bowl. Add in the remaining ingredients. Serves 5.

HEAVY METALS BE GONE SOUP

1   avocado
1   red bell pepper
1   ripe tomato
1   lemon (seeds removed to avoid bitterness)
1   bunch cilantro
1   bunch cilantro
1   ripe tomato, chopped
1   carrot, grated
1   handful dulse leaves, chopped
1   cup sunflower sprouts, chopped

Blend first 5 thoroughly and pour out into a bowl. Add in the remaining ingredients. Serves 4.

BORSCHT

2 cups water
3 beets
1 small gingerroot, sliced
3–4 large cloves garlic
6–7 bay leaves
2 cups water
2 carrots
2 stalks celery
1 tablespoon apple cider vinegar
3 oranges, peeled with seeds removed (the seeds are very bitter)
1 tablespoon honey
¼ cup olive oil
1 teaspoon sea salt
½ cup walnuts
¼ head cabbage, grated
1–2 carrots, grated
½ bunch parsley, chopped

Blend the first 5 ingredients well in a blender Pour the mixture into a big bowl. Blend the next 9 ingredients at a low speed for about 30 seconds to break ingredients into small pieces but not pulverize them completely. Combine with beet mixture and stir. Add parsley and grated ingredients to the mixture, stir it up, and serve. Serves 5–6.

CHILI

2 cups fresh tomatoes
1 cup water
1 cup dried tomatoes

1	cup sprouted lentils
1	bunch fresh basil, chopped
½	cup raisins
½	cup extra-virgin olive oil
¼	cup lemon juice
1	habañero
2–5	cloves garlic
1	heaping tablespoon cumin

Blend all ingredients except sprouted lentils and basil in a blender for 2 minutes. Pour chili into a bowl and mix in sprouted lentils. Sprinkle basil on top. Serves 5–7.

THAI SOUP

2	cucumbers, peeled
2	cups water
½	cup walnuts
¼	cup Nama Shoyu
½	fresh spicy pepper
1	teaspoon salt
2	tablespoons honey
¼	cup chopped ginger
¼	cup lemon juice
½	teaspoon turmeric
1	cucumber, peeled and thinly sliced
½	cup dried mushrooms
1	bunch cilantro, chopped

Blend first ten ingredients in a blender until smooth. Add remaining ingredients and stir well. Enjoy! Serves 5.

CREAM OF CELERY SOUP

1	medium bunch celery, chopped
3	cups water
¼	cup olive oil
¼	cup lemon juice
1	tablespoon honey
	spicy pepper to taste
	teaspoon sea salt
1	avocado, thinly sliced
1	small sweet red pepper, chopped

Blend first 6 ingredients in a blender until creamy. Add avocado and sweet pepper. Serves 5.

SEA VEGETABLE SOUP

1	cup almonds
3	cups water
¼	cup olive oil
¼	cup lemon juice
2	tablespoons raw honey
3	bay leaves
1	teaspoon sea salt
	chile pepper to taste
2	nori sheets, torn into small squares
2	tablespoons dulse flakes
¼	cup dry arame (soaked in water 10 minutes)

Blend first 8 ingredients in a blender until smooth. Add remaining ingredients into the soup and let stand for 20 minutes. Serves 4–5.

GAZPACHO

½	cup water
¼	cup extra-virgin olive oil

5	large ripe tomatoes
2	cloves garlic or spicy pepper to taste
1	tablespoon raw honey (dates or raisins work just as well)
¼	cup lemon juice
1	teaspoon sea salt
1	bunch fresh basil
1	large avocado
1	medium bell pepper
5	stalks celery
1	small onion
1	generous pinch parsley, chopped

Blend the first 8 ingredients in a blender until smooth. Cut the avocado, bell pepper, celery, and onion into ½-inch pieces and combine with gazpacho liquid in a bowl. Sprinkle with parsley and serve. Serves 4–5.

RED AND SPICY SOUP

In a blender, blend:

1–1½	cup pine nuts
¼	cup olive oil
½	lemon, juiced
6	small tomatoes (cherry or other)
4–5	cloves garlic
1–2	fresh cayenne peppers
1	teaspoon sea salt
½	bunch thyme

Blend well and stir in small chunks of avocado, cucumber, and red and yellow bell pepper. Serves 3.

DILL-ICIOUS SOUP

3	large fresh tomatoes
2–3	cloves garlic
½	bunch dill
1	cup water
⅓	cup lemon juice
1	teaspoon sea salt
¼	cup olive oil
¼	cup raisins
½	cup dried tomatoes
1	avocado, finely chopped
1	bell pepper, finely chopped

Blend the first 9 ingredients well in a blender. Combine the avocado and bell pepper with the blended ingredients and garnish the soup with dill. Serves 3–4.

DILL-LIGHTFUL SOUP

2	cups coconut water
1	avocado
1	stalk celery
1	stalk rhubarb
½	bunch fresh dill

Blend all ingredients in a blender until smooth. Serve chilled and garnished with dill. Serves 4.

GINGER SOUP

½	cup pecans
2	cups coconut milk

2	finger-sized ginger pieces, diced
½	bunch fresh basil
1	hot pepper, diced
½	teaspoon salt
¼	cup lemon juice
½	cucumber
½	bell pepper
½	avocado
2	tablespoons dehydrated sweet onion

Blend the first 7 ingredients in a Vita-Mix and pour into a bowl. Coarsely chop remaining ingredients and combine with blended mixture. Garnish with edible flowers and dill. Serves 4–5. See plate 14.

UN-CHICKEN NOODLE SOUP

Blend together:

2	cups water
½	cup walnuts or pecans
¼	cup olive oil
1	cup celery, chopped
2	tablespoons Nama Shoyu
2–3	cloves of garlic
	pepper to taste (optional)
1	medium carrot, grated
½	bunch parsley, chopped
2	medium raw potatoes, grated or processed with a spiralizer

Add the celery, Nama Shoyu, garlic, and pepper and blend for about 1 minute. Pour into a large bowl and add remaining ingredients. Serves 7. See plate 13.

Entrées

Since an entrée is the main course, it must live up to high expectations. By the time the entrée is served, the diners have already consumed an appetizer or salad and are eagerly anticipating what's next. Presenting your main course in a visually appealing manner will increase the intensity of the flavors and overall meal satisfaction for your dinner guests. In our first year of eating raw foods, our mother learned by trial and error that making food look beautiful was half the battle in getting her kids and husband to eat raw food. Upon presenting an ungarnished dinner in an old, dull bowl, she noticed that, despite our hunger, her family wasn't all that eager to eat. The next time she prepared dinner, she replaced the old bowls with bright new ones, laid out the garden burger on a bed of lettuce, and garnished her creation with seasonal fresh veggies. This time, the whole family enjoyed the meal, leaving not even a morsel of leftovers. In this section, you will find many delicious ideas for main courses. Consider how you can decorate your creations so that even someone with other food preferences will be dazzled and excited to devour it!

DILL BURGERS

1	cup flaxseeds
½	pounds dry almonds
½	bunch green onions
½	pounds carrots
1	large tomato
1	large bunch fresh dill
4–5	cloves garlic
¼	cup onion powder
¼	cup lemon juice
¼	cup olive oil
1–2	teaspoons salt

Using a blender or coffee grinder, grind the flaxseeds to a powder. Process the almonds in the food processor and combine with the flaxseeds. Dice the green onions, and mix with almonds and flaxseeds. Process the remaining ingredients in the food processor for 1 minute. Mix all ingredients thoroughly. Scoop out mixture, flatten into patties, and dry on dehydrator trays for 12–14 hours at 110°. Flip burgers and continue drying for 5–8 hours. Yields approximately 12 burgers.

HOMEGROWN SANDWICH

BREAD

1   cup flaxseeds, ground
1   medium onion, chopped
3   cloves garlic
½–1 cup water
½–1 teaspoon sea salt

Grind the flaxseeds in a Vita-Mix blender or coffee grinder and transfer it into a bowl. Blend remaining ingredients in a food processor and mix with flaxseeds. Spread mixture onto dehydrator trays and dry for 16–20 hours at 110°.

PÂTÉ

1   cup almonds, soaked 8 hours
3   carrots, chopped
2   stalks celery, chopped
1   medium onion, chopped
2   cloves garlic
2   tablespoons olive oil
½   lemon, juiced
1   teaspoon sea salt

Blend all ingredients in a food processor until mixed thoroughly. Spread pâté on bread and fill with your favorite vegetables, for example, lettuce, tomato, onion, or red bell pepper. Garnish sandwich with seasonal veggies or fruits. Note: olives go well with this combination. Yields 3–5 sandwiches.

CASHEW GARDEN BURGERS

2   cups cashews
1   cup dried tomatoes (soaked in water 10 minutes)
¼   bunch cilantro
2   tablespoons olive oil
½   teaspoon sea salt

Blend all ingredients in a food processor. If necessary add water from dried tomatoes to help blend the ingredients. Scoop out mixture, flatten into patties, and dry on dehydrator trays for 10–12 hours at 110°. Then flip and continue drying for 5–8 hours. Yields approximately 5 burgers.

FRUIT SUSHI ROLLS

PÂTÉ

1   cup sunflower seeds, soaked 8 hours
3   carrots, chopped
1   small red onion, chopped
2   tablespoons olive oil
1   teaspoon Nama Shoyu
½   lemon, juiced
1   teaspoon sea salt
1   mango, sliced thin
1   medium avocado, sliced thin
1   carrot, peeled and sliced thin
½   cup alfalfa or radish sprouts

Blend the first 7 ingredients in a food processor for 1 minute.

WASABI

1   tablespoon hot wasabi power
½   teaspoon Nama Shoyu

Spread sunflower pâté onto a crispy sheet of nori. Add a proportionate amount of sliced mango, avocado, carrot, and sprouts atop pâté. Carefully roll up ingredients into nori sheet. Wait for nori sheet to bind before slicing. Mix wasabi ingredients in a small dish to a creamy consistency. Serve the sushi rolls with fresh fruit and wasabi. Yields 3–4 rolls.

GORILLA BURGERS

GARDEN BURGER INGREDIENTS

1	cup walnuts
¼	flaxseeds, ground
3	carrots, chopped
1	medium red onion, chopped
2	cloves garlic
½	lime, juiced
1	tablespoon onion powder
1	teaspoon paprika
1	teaspoon sea salt

ADDITIONAL INGREDIENTS

1	head romaine lettuce (leaves cut away from stem)
1	large tomato, chopped
½	bunch green onions, diced
½	avocado, sliced thin

Blend all garden burger ingredients in a food processor. Fill romaine leaves with garden burger. Add tomato chunks and onions and top with avocado slices. Serve with "Raw Ketchup" (page 73). Serves 3–4.

LIVE GARDEN BURGER

2	cups almonds
3	carrots, coarsely chopped
1	medium onion, coarsely chopped
¼	cup raisins
1	teaspoon honey
1–2	tablespoons olive oil
¼	bunch fresh herbs (such as basil, thyme, dill, rosemary)
1	teaspoon sea salt

Blend all ingredients in a food processor. Form into balls, cutlets, or fillets and sprinkle with a little paprika. Dehydrate for authentic garden burger look or eat as is, pâté-like. Serve with salad or veggies on the side. Serves 6–7.

PORTOBELLO MUSHROOM BURGER

2	cups cashews
3	carrots, coarsely chopped
1	medium red onion, coarsely chopped
¼	cup raisins or dates
1	teaspoon honey
1–2	tablespoons olive oil
¼	bunch fresh dill
1	teaspoon sea salt
1	teaspoon balsamic vinegar

Blend all ingredients in a food processor. Prepare portobello mushrooms by cutting out their stems. Fill mushrooms with pâté. Add any of the following to complete the burger: tomato, red bell pepper, onion, lettuce, olives, chives, sprouts, and some kind of savory sauce. Cover burger with leaf of lettuce or another mushroom. Garnish with herbs and serve with a side of veggies. Serves 4–5. See plate 11.

NORI ROLLS

PÂTÉ MIXTURE

½	cup walnuts
1	cup sunflower seeds, soaked overnight
3	garlic cloves
1	cup chopped celery
1	teaspoon salt
¼	cup olive oil
¼	cup lemon juice
1	tablespoon lemongrass, chopped
½	avocado
½	large bell pepper
2	green onions
5	raw nori sheets

Blend the first 8 ingredients in a food processor. Slice the remaining ingredients into long, extra-thin slices. Spread the pâté onto a sheet of nori and add the thinly sliced vegetables. For a nice visual touch, let sliced vegetables stick out from sides of nori rolls before rolling. Tightly roll pâté with veggies into nori sheets. Wait 10 minutes and then begin slicing the nori rolls into 2-inch slices. Note: to make the nori sheets stick better, moisten them a little with water or lemon, tomato, or orange juice. Yields 5–6 rolls. See plate 12.

VALYA'S SUNFLOWER TORTE

This savory torte looks very impressive when finished.

4	cups sunflower seeds
1	large white onion
1	bunch Italian parsley
2	cloves garlic
¼	cup lemon juice
¼	cup olive oil
1	teaspoon salt
1	tomato, sliced

Grind first 7 ingredients in a food processor and mix thoroughly.
Make a layer of pâté on a plate. For the next layer, use sliced
tomatoes. Last but not least, spread another layer of pâté on top of
the tomatoes. Serves 4–5.

RAW-KIN LIVE PIZZA

CRUST

2	cups golden flaxseeds, ground
1	cup water
1	large red onion, coarsely chopped
2	large yellow tomatoes
4–5	cloves garlic
¼	bunch fresh basil
1–2	tablespoons olive oil
1–2	tablespoons honey
1	teaspoon sea salt

Grind flaxseeds in Vita-Mix blender or coffee grinder. Blend all
remaining ingredients in a food processor and mix with flaxseeds.
Spread onto dehydrator trays in desired shape and dry for 16 hours
at 110°. Flip pizza and continue drying for 5–7 hours at 110°. See
plate 9.

1   cup cashews
¼   cup lemon juice
1–2 tablespoons olive oil
1–2 tablespoons nutritional yeast

Spread cheese onto pizza crust.

TOPPING

½   cup dried tomatoes, soaked in water 10 minutes
1   large, ripe tomato, chopped
¼   bunch fresh basil
½   lemon, juiced
1   tablespoon olive oil
1   tablespoon honey
1   teaspoon sea salt

Blend all ingredients in a food processor until creamy. Pour topping over pizza. Garnish with any or all of the following: olives, onions, dried mushrooms, bell peppers, cherry tomatoes, or basil leaves. Serves 6.

CRUNCH FRIES

They look as real as if purchased at the drive-through window.

1   pound jicama (sliced in french-fry shapes)
1   tablespoon onion powder
2   tablespoons extra-virgin olive oil
     sea salt to taste
1   tablespoon paprika

In a bowl, combine jicama with remaining ingredients. Mix thoroughly. Serve with "Raw Ketchup" (page 73). Serves 3–4. See plate 11.

BETTER THAN REAL BURRITOS

*We honestly thought we would never eat anything that
resembled a real burrito again until we invented this dish.*

BREAD

Follow the recipe for "Igor's Crackers" (page 175). Dehydrate
them only halfway. They are ready when they feel soft. Note: the
possibilities with soft crackers are endless. You can wrap them
around or stuff them with anything, so experiment!

PÂTÉ

    3   cups almonds
    5–6   cups water

Blend these ingredients in a blender until smooth and strain
through a nut-milk bag. Take the almond pulp and add:

    ½   cup green onion, finely chopped
    1   bunch fresh dill, chopped
    ¼   cup olive oil
    ¼   cup lemon or lime juice
    2   teaspoons sea salt

Sprinkle with cayenne pepper to taste. Spread as much pâté as you
desire on the bread. Add chopped veggies and roll the mixture onto
the cracker. If necessary, use a toothpick to pin down the burrito to
prevent unraveling.

SPAGHETTI

*Even the color of the noodle strands resembles the real thing,
and the sauce is to live for!*

Using a shredder or spiralizer, shred a desired amount of any of
the following veggies: butternut squash, rutabaga, turnip, carrot,
yellow beet, or celery root.

TOMATO-BASIL SAUCE

1   cup fresh chopped tomatoes
2–3 cloves garlic
½   cup fresh basil, chopped
1   medium lemon, juiced
2   tablespoons olive oil
4   dates (or some raisins)
1   cup dried tomatoes
½   teaspoon sea salt

Blend all ingredients. Serves 3–4.

TURKEYLESS TURKEY

We have fun with this dish on Thanksgiving Day.

½   pound almonds, soaked overnight
½   pound walnuts, soaked overnight
1   pound carrots, finely grated
1   medium onion, diced
¼   cup raisins
1–2 tablespoons coconut oil
1   teaspoon caraway seeds, ground
1   tablespoon Italian seasoning
      sea salt to taste

Run all ingredients through a Champion juicer using the blank plate or mix in a food processor. If the mixture is not firm enough, add one or a couple of the following thickeners: dried garlic, dried onion, dried parsley flakes, nutritional yeast, or ground flaxseeds. Form into patties and dry in a food dehydrator for 16–18 hours at 110°. Sprinkle with paprika or ground black pepper before serving. Serves 8–10.

INSTEAD OF MASHED POTATOES

If you want to make something quick and yummy, this is the dish for you! We prepare it not only for Thanksgiving but year-round!

2	large avocados
½	head cauliflower
¼	cup lemon juice
¼	cup sweet onion powder
1	teaspoon sea salt

Blend all ingredients in a food processor. Use as a side dish or main course. Serves 3–4.

THREE

Desserts

CAKES AND PIES

Welcome to the exciting world of raw desserts! Of all the different types of raw-food recipes, raw cakes and pies are our favorites. We like to think of each of our pies as a creative masterpiece. Just as a painter carefully chooses her color palette prior to starting a painting, so do we when choosing the colorful ingredients for our pies. Just as an artist makes every motion of the paintbrush with meticulous precision, we too strive for perfection. Finally, in the same manner that an artist adds his finishing touches, we garnish our cakes and pies with ripe berries, fresh herbs, and exotic spices. We invite you to see how creative you can be with your sweet tooth.

APRICOT COBBLER

CRUST

1½   cups buckwheat, ground
1   cup rolled oats, ground
3   apricots
2   tablespoons agave nectar

Blend apricots with agave nectar in food processor and mix with oats and buckwheat to form crust. Spread piecrust on an appetizing plate or platter in a desired shape or thickness.

FILLING

6   medium apricots
½   cup agave nectar

Blend filling ingredients in a blender until smooth. Spread on top of piecrust and garnish with your favorite fruit. Chill in freezer prior to serving. Serves 5.

VALYA'S SECRET GOOSEBERRY CHEESECAKE

CRUST

4   cups almond pulp (from "Almond Milk" recipe, page 151)
2   tablespoons agave nectar
¼   cup fresh gooseberries

Blend ingredients in food processor. Form a pie-like crust in your favorite pie dish. *Note:* set enough crust aside to cover the top of the cake filling.

FILLING

2   cups gooseberries
⅓   cup agave nectar

Blend ingredients in a blender. Transfer filling into pie dish and cover with remaining crust. Garnish with your favorite fruit and serve. Serves 4–5.

ALMOND CAKE

This cake looks professional and is easy to cut.

CRUST

3	cups ground almonds
1	tablespoon olive oil
¼	cup honey
½	teaspoon salt
½	cup chopped or crushed dates, presoaked 1–2 hours
1	teaspoon vanilla extract
¼	cup raw carob powder
4	tangerine peels, chopped

Grind ingredients in a food processor and mix well. If mixture is not firm enough, add psyllium husk or shredded coconut. Form into crust on a flat plate.

TOPPING

½	cup almonds
½	cup olive oil
2–3	tablespoons honey
1	medium lemon, juiced
1	teaspoon vanilla

Blend topping ingredients well, adding water with a teaspoon if necessary. Spread topping evenly over the crust. Garnish with fruits, berries, and nuts. Chill before serving. Serves 5. See plate 15.

SWEET PURPLE SEED CHEESE

5   cups soaked sunflower seeds
1   cup fresh blueberries
1   cup fresh blackberries
¼   cup agave nectar
1   apple, sliced

Blend the sunflower seeds in a blender. Pour the contents out into a nut-milk bag and hang the bag for 5 hours to drip off the excess water and slightly ferment the cheese. Then dump the contents of the nut-milk bag into a bowl and mix in the remaining ingredients. Serve on apple slices. Serves 7.

CHOCOLATE CREAM PIE

CRUST

2   cups macadamia nuts
1   cup dried pineapple
3–4 dates, pitted
⅕   teaspoon sea salt

Blend all ingredients in food processor until thoroughly mixed. Sprinkle some crushed nut pieces onto a clean plate or pie pan to prevent crust from sticking to plate surface so you can easily separate the finished cake. Form blended mixture into desired piecrust shape.

CREAM

1   young coconut (meat and water)
½   cup cacao nibs
½   cup dates, pitted

2	tablespoons coconut butter
1	tablespoon vanilla extract

Blend all ingredients in blender for 3 minutes or until smooth. Transfer blended mixture into piecrust. With a spatula, spread the cream evenly throughout the crust. Garnish with fresh mint leaves and seasonal fruit. Serves 6–7.

PEAR PIE

CRUST

2	ripe pears, peeled and thinly sliced
2	cups hazelnuts (not soaked)
1	cup dried blueberries
¼	cup apple cider

Blend all ingredients except fresh pears in food processor until thoroughly mixed. Sprinkle some crushed nut pieces onto a clean plate or pie pan to prevent crust from sticking to plate surface so you can easily separate the finished cake. Form blended mixture into desired piecrust shape. Spread sliced pears evenly on top of piecrust.

CREAM

1	young coconut (meat and water)
1	ripe pear, peeled and chopped
2	tablespoons agar agar (a natural thickener)
½	cup dried pears (soaked 15 minutes)

Blend all ingredients in blender for 3 minutes or until smooth. Transfer blended mixture into piecrust. With a spatula, spread the cream evenly throughout the crust. Garnish with seasonal fruit and fresh herbs. Chill before serving. Serves 6–7.

MULBERRY PIE

CRUST

2	cups macadamia nuts (not soaked)
1	cup dates, pitted
½	lime, sliced with peel
1	tablespoon honey
½	teaspoon cinnamon
⅕	teaspoon sea salt

Blend all ingredients in food processor until thoroughly mixed. Sprinkle some crushed nut pieces onto a clean plate or pie pan to prevent crust from sticking to plate surface so you can easily separate the finished cake. Form blended mixture into desired piecrust shape.

CREAM

1–2	pints fresh mulberries
½	cup prunes, soaked 15 minutes
1	fresh mango, pitted, peeled, and chopped

Blend all ingredients in blender for 3 minutes or until smooth. Transfer blended mixture into piecrust. With a spatula, spread the cream evenly throughout the crust. Garnish with fresh mint leaves and seasonal fruit. Serves 6–7.

COCONUT CREAM PIE

CRUST

1	cup cashews (not soaked)
1	cup macadamia nuts (not soaked)
1	cup golden raisins
5–6	dried figs
⅕	teaspoon sea salt

Blend all ingredients in food processor until thoroughly mixed. Sprinkle some crushed nut pieces onto a clean plate or pie pan to prevent crust from sticking to plate surface so you can easily separate the finished cake. Form blended mixture into desired piecrust shape.

CREAM

2   large young coconuts (meat and water)
4   tablespoons agar agar (a natural thickener)
2–3   tablespoons honey
½   lime, juiced
1   teaspoon caramel extract

Blend all ingredients in blender for 3 minutes or until smooth. Transfer blended mixture into piecrust. With a spatula, spread the cream evenly throughout the crust. Garnish with thinly sliced lemon peel. Chill before serving. Serves 6–7. See plate 17.

MANGO PUDDING PIE

CRUST

2   cups pistachios (not soaked)
1   cup dried golden mulberries
½   lemon, juiced
2–3   drops lemon essential oil

Blend all ingredients in food processor until thoroughly mixed. Sprinkle some crushed nut pieces onto a clean plate or pie pan to prevent crust from sticking to plate surface so you can easily separate the finished cake. Form blended mixture into desired piecrust shape.

CREAM

2   ripe mangoes, peeled, pitted, and chopped

Blend chopped mangoes in a blender without adding any water. This creates a thick creamy layer. Spread on top of piecrust. Garnish pie with blueberries and fresh lavender. Serves 5–6.

PEACH PERFECTION

CRUST

2	cups almonds (not soaked)
1	cup hemp seeds (not soaked)
1	cup raisins
1	ripe banana
1	teaspoon vanilla extract
1/5	teaspoon salt

Blend all ingredients in food processor until thoroughly mixed. Sprinkle some crushed nut pieces onto a clean plate or pie pan to prevent crust from sticking to plate surface so you can easily separate the finished cake. Form blended mixture into desired piecrust shape.

CREAM

2	ripe peaches, chopped
2–3	tablespoons agar agar (natural thickener)
2	tablespoons honey
1	teaspoon vanilla extract

Blend all ingredients in blender for 3 minutes or until smooth. Transfer blended mixture into piecrust. With a spatula, spread the cream evenly throughout the crust. Garnish with fresh jasmine petals, strawberries, and fresh mint. Serves 6–7.

POPULAR PAPAYA PIE

CRUST

2	cups pecans (not soaked)
1	cup pine nuts (not soaked)
1	cup apricots

1   teaspoon caramel extract
⅕   teaspoon sea salt

Blend all ingredients in food processor until thoroughly mixed.
Sprinkle some crushed nut pieces onto a clean plate or pie pan
to prevent crust from sticking to plate surface so you can easily
separate the finished cake. Form blended mixture into desired
piecrust shape.

CREAM

1   ripe strawberry papaya, peeled, seeded, and
      chopped
2–3   tablespoons agar agar (natural thickener)
¼   cup apple cider
1   tablespoon coconut butter
3–4   dates, pitted
1   tablespoon vanilla extract

Blend all ingredients in blender for 3 minutes or until smooth.
Transfer blended mixture into piecrust. With a spatula, spread the
cream evenly throughout the crust. Garnish with fresh mint leaves
and seasonal fruit. Chill before serving. Serves 6–7.

COLD Desserts

We have always been fascinated by cold desserts. As children, we
loved eating ice cream, especially chocolate. Since our first day eating raw food, we have been inspired to create a frozen imitation of
the childhood food that we loved so much. It took many tries, but we
are proud to say that we have succeeded!

CHOCOLATE CHEESE

6   cups sunflower seeds, soaked overnight
4   cups water

Blend sunflower seeds with water and pour into nut-milk bag. Hang for 5 hours. Mix with the following ingredients:

5   tablespoons raw cacao powder
1/3 cup agave nectar

Combine mixtures, chill, and serve with fruit. Serves 5.

HEAVENLY CHOCOLATE

1   cup raw cashews or macadamia-nut butter
1/4 cup water
3   tablespoons honey
2   tablespoons carob powder
1   teaspoon vanilla
1/4 teaspoon sea salt

Blend well, pour into a flat dish, and freeze until solid. Serves 3–4.

CARAMEL

7   Brazil nuts
5   tablespoons agave nectar
4   tablespoons cacao butter
1/2 teaspoon cacao powder
1/5 teaspoon salt

Blend until smooth. Pour into a flat dish and freeze until solid. Serves 6.

ENERGY GEL

½   cup cacao beans
1   tablespoon coconut oil
¼   cup goji berries
¼   teaspoon sea salt
1   tablespoon honey
1   teaspoon spirulina (Hawaiian algae)

Blend all ingredients in blender for 20 minutes or until smooth. Chill in refrigerator. Eat when you need an energy boost. Serves 2.

CHOCOHOLIC'S DELIGHT

¼   cup cacao nibs
1   avocado
¼   cup dates, pitted
¼   teaspoon sea salt
2   tablespoons agave nectar
1   thumb-size piece of fresh ginger, peeled and diced

Blend all ingredients in blender for 2 minutes or until smooth. Chill and eat. Serves 3.

CHOCOLATE FRENZY

½   cup cacao butter
4   tablespoons raw cacao powder
5   tablespoons agave nectar
5   Brazil nuts
⅕   teaspoon salt

Blend thoroughly and enjoy. You can store this heavenly bliss in the freezer. See plate 16.

CACAO PUDDING

5   ripe avocados
¾   cups Ultimate Raw cacao powder (brand)
1   teaspoon vanilla extract
1   teaspoon cider vinegar
1   pinch sea salt (optional)
¼   cup water
1   cup Ultimate Raw agave nectar (brand)

Place avocados in food processor and pulverize; add in cacao powder, vanilla, apple cider vinegar, water, and salt. Mix together to creamy consistency. Add sweetener as desired. Chill and serve. Serves 5. See plate 18. (This recipe is by Richard Homsley of Synergy Chef Collaborative.)

CHOCOLATE DIRT

½   cup coconut butter
5   tablespoons raw cacao powder
2   tablespoons honey
½   teaspoon vanilla extract
¼   teaspoon salt
⅕   teaspoon nutmeg

Mix together and serve in small piles atop sliced fruit. Serves 5.

candies and energy bars

As more scientific research hits the mainstream about the health benefits of eating fresh, more athletes are reevaluating their diets and choosing the healthier alternative. Raw candies and energy bars are surfacing in all major health food stores, as well as large whole-sale stores such as Costco and Sam's Club. While these products are delicious, they pack a punch to the wallet, with prices reaching nine dollars for a single bar. We offer many energy-rich recipes to help you keep going strong, whether you are climbing a mountain or running errands. Best of all, every ingredient we use to make these yummy treats is inexpensive and easy to find, which means that the end product will cost less than a tenth of the price of a store-bought bar. Now that's something to get energetic about!

ENERGY NUGGETS

1   cup Brazil nuts
1   cup hazelnuts
½   cup dried blueberries
1   fresh persimmon
¼   cup raisins
1–2   tablespoons agave nectar
      carob powder or coconut flakes to taste

Blend first 6 ingredients in food processor until thoroughly mixed. Roll mixture into small nuggets. Finish by rolling in carob powder or coconut flakes. Serves 4–5.

WATERMELON CANDY

1   cup lemon juice
1   medium watermelon, peeled and thinly sliced

Pour lemon juice over sliced watermelon. Spread out onto dehydrator trays. Dry for 12–18 hours at 110° or until fully dried. Serves 10.

GOJI BAR

1	pound almonds (not soaked)
½	cup goji berries
6–8	dates, pitted
2	tablespoons agave nectar
1	tablespoon orange extract
¼	teaspoon sea salt

Blend all ingredients in food processor in short bursts. The object is to mix all ingredients without pulverizing the food. Take about a handful of the mixture and use your hands to form it into a rectangular bar shape. Repeat this process until blended mixture runs out. Place bars in freezer for 1 hour for better shape. This will also reduce surface stickiness. Yields 10 bars.

MULBERRY BAR

1	pound hazelnuts (not soaked)
½	cup died golden mulberries
¼	cup shredded coconut
2	tablespoons agave nectar
1	tablespoon vanilla extract
¼	teaspoon sea salt

Blend all ingredients in food processor in short bursts. The object is to mix all ingredients without pulverizing the food. Take about a handful of mixture and use your hands to form it into a rectangular bar shape. Repeat process until blended mixture runs out. Place bars in freezer for 1 hour for better shape. This will also reduce surface stickiness. Yields 10 bars.

BANANA BARS

1   pound of macadamia nuts (unsoaked)
2–3   ripe bananas
½   cup raisins
½   lime, peeled and juiced
2   tablespoons organic date sugar

Blend all ingredients in food processor for 2 minutes or until thoroughly mixed. Take about a handful of mixture and use your hands to form it into a rectangular bar shape. Repeat process until blended mixture runs out. Place bars on dehydrator trays and dry at 110° for 10–14 hours. Yields 10 bars.

BLUEBERRY MANGO BALLS

1   cup dried mango pieces, chopped and soaked in water 15 minutes
1   cup dried blueberries
1   cup coconut flakes
½   cup pine nuts
⅕   teaspoon sea salt
      carob powder or coconut flakes to taste

Blend first 5 ingredients in food processor for 2 minutes or until thoroughly mixed. Take about a tablespoon of the mixture and roll it into a ball shape. Repeat process until blended mixture runs out. The balls can be rolled in shredded coconut or carob powder, or frozen to reduce surface stickiness. Yields 15–18 balls.

SIMPLE BUT DELIGHTFUL

1   pound cashews (not soaked)
½   cup dates, pitted
2   tablespoons honey
2   heaping tablespoons carob powder
¼   teaspoon sea salt
        carob powder or coconut flakes to taste

Blend first 5 ingredients in food processor for 2 minutes or until thoroughly mixed. Take about a tablespoon of the mixture and roll it into a ball shape. Repeat process until blended mixture runs out. The balls can be rolled in shredded coconut or carob powder, or frozen to reduce surface stickiness. Yields 15–18 balls.

CHOCO-WALNUT BAR

1 pound walnuts (not soaked)
½ cup dates, pitted
½ cup dried cherries
¼ cup cacao nibs
1 tablespoon honey
⅕ teaspoon sea salt

Blend all ingredients in food processor in short bursts. The object is to mix all ingredients without pulverizing the food. Take about a handful of the mixture and use your hands to form it into a rectangular bar shape. Repeat process until blended mixture runs out. Place bars in freezer for 1 hour for better shape. This will also reduce surface stickiness. Yields 10 bars.

CASHEW COOKIE BAR

1   pound cashews (not soaked)
1   cup dates, pitted
1   cup dried cherries
1   teaspoon caramel extract
1/5 teaspoon sea salt

Blend all ingredients in food processor in short bursts. The object is to mix all ingredients without pulverizing the food. Take about a handful of mixture and use your hands to form it into a rectangular bar shape. Repeat process until blended mixture runs out. Place bars in freezer for 1 hour for better shape. This will also reduce surface stickiness. Yields 10 bars.

SWEET AND SOUR COCONUT TRUFFLES

1   pound coconut flakes
1   cup dried cranberries
1   cup pine nuts
2   tablespoons honey
1/5 teaspoon sea salt
     carob powder or coconut flakes to taste

Blend first 5 ingredients in food processor for 2 minutes or until thoroughly mixed. Take about a tablespoon of the mixture and roll it into a ball shape. Repeat process until blended mixture runs out. The balls can be rolled in shredded coconut or carob powder, or frozen to reduce surface stickiness. Yields 15 balls.

PEACH COBBLER BAR

1	pound almonds (not soaked)
1	cup dried peaches, chopped and soaked 15 minutes
½	cup dates, pitted
2	tablespoons agave nectar
1	tablespoon vanilla extract
1	teaspoon powdered cinnamon
⅕	teaspoon sea salt

Blend all ingredients in food processor in short bursts. The object is to mix all ingredients without pulverizing the food. Take about a handful of the mixture and use your hands to form it into a rectangular bar shape. Repeat process until blended mixture runs out. Place bars in freezer for 1 hour for better shape. This will also reduce surface stickiness. Yields 10 bars.

CRANBERRY-GINGER BAR

1	pound pecans (not soaked)
1	cup dried cranberries
½	cup golden raisins
1	thumb-sized piece ginger, peeled and minced
2	tablespoons honey
1	teaspoon orange extract
⅕	teaspoon sea salt

Blend all ingredients in food processor in short bursts. The object is to mix all ingredients without pulverizing the food. Take about a handful of the mixture and use your hands to form it into a rectangular bar shape. Repeat process until blended mixture runs out. Place bars in freezer for 1 hour for better shape. This will also reduce surface stickiness. Yields 10 bars.

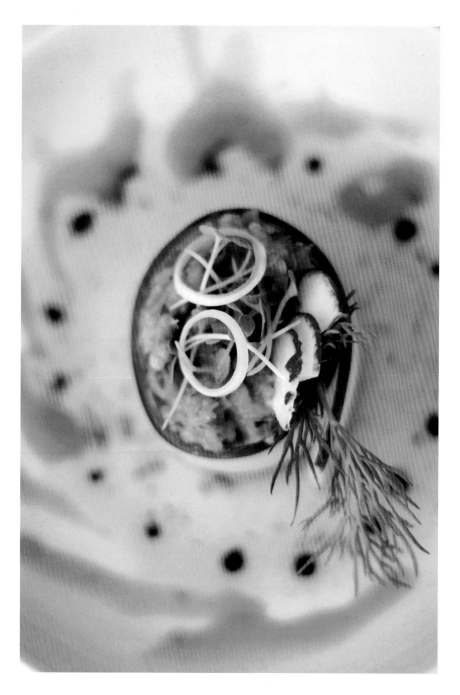

1   Cucumber Yam Salad Rolls. See recipe, page 60.

RECIPES, EXOTIC FRUITS, AND WILD EDIBLES

2   Barley Salad Yam Wrap. See recipe, page 69.

3   Microgreen Salad. See recipe, page 67.

RECIPES, EXOTIC FRUITS, AND WILD EDIBLES

4   Spicy Tomato Salad with Garden Burger Pâté. See recipes, pages 62 and 88.

5   I Can't Believe It's Just Cabbage Salad and Marinated Kale Salad. See recipes, pages 62 ans 64.

6   Golden Flax Crackers and Cloud Chips. See recipes, pages 173 and 178.

7   Rosemary Endive Salad. See recipe, page 69.

RECIPES, EXOTIC FRUITS, AND WILD EDIBLES

8   Live Garden Burger. See recipe, page 88.

9   Raw-kin Live Pizza. See recipe, page 90.

RECIPES, EXOTIC FRUITS, AND WILD EDIBLES

10 Garden Burger with Sauerkraut and Golden Flax Crackers. See recipes, pages 88, 158, 173.

11 Portobello Mushroom Burger with Crunch Fries and Raw Ketchup. See recipes, pages 88, 91, and 73.

12   Nori Rolls. See recipe, page 89.

13   Un-chicken Noodle Soup. See recipe, page 83.

14   Ginger Soup. See recipe, page 82.

15   Almond Cake. See recipe, page 97.

16   Chocolate Frenzy. See recipe, page 105.

17   Coconut Cream Pie. See recipe, page 100.

18   Cacao Pudding, Strawberry-Coconut Pudding, and Date with a Coconut.
See recipes, pages 106, 129, 142.

19   Cashew-Orange Thumbprints. See recipe, page 118.

20   The papaya is native to Mexico. When this fruit is ripe, it feels soft (like a ripe avocado or a bit softer) and its skin has attained an amber to orange color. Papaya tastes similar to the combination of a pineapple and a peach and has the texture of an over-ripe cataloupe.

21   Papaya is eaten with seeds removed.

22   Native to Mexico and Central and South America, dragonfruit is a cactus fruit with a leathery, slightly leafy pink skin. Its white meat is mildly sweet, low in calories, and similar in texture to a kiwi. The skin is not eaten.

23   Dragonfruit is rich in fiber, vitamin C, and minerals. It is served sliced or in fruit salads.

24   Lychee is native to Southern China. The outside is covered by a pink-red, roughly-textured rind that is inedible but easily removed. The inside consists of a layer of sweet, translucent white flesh, rich in vitamin C, with a texture somewhat similar to that of a grape. The center contains a single glossy brown nut-like seed. The seed is slightly poisonous and should not be eaten.

25   Durian is a big, thorny fruit from Southeast Asia. It is considered to be "the king of fruit" throughout Thailand. Durian is famous for both its delicious taste and stinky smell. The pods are filled with a sweet, creamy, custard-like, white meat. Durians taste best when locally available and eaten fresh, but are also available frozen.

26   Put the fresh or defrosted durian on a cutting board. When handling a durian, always use a folded towel to protect your hands from the sharp spikes. Make a long, slightly curved cut along one of the five bumpy lobes. Cut approximately 1/2 inch deep, just through the shell. Make another curved cut along the other side of the same lobe. These two cuts should create an oval.

27   Once these two cuts have been made, lift up the oval piece of shell and use a spoon to remove custard from the pod.

28   Mangoes are native to India. They are a very sweet fruit, containing up to 15 percent sugar. Mangoes are packed with vitamins A, B, C, E and P, as well as calcium, iron, potassium, and magnesium. Mangoes have a large flat pit inside. For this reason, they are shaped like a slightly squished oval. The widest part of the mango is where the flat pit is located.

29   To get the most meat, slice off the flatter sides of the fruit as close to the pit as possible. Your goal is to cut off most of the mango meat in these two cuts. There will be some meat still on the pit, which you may cut off separately with a small paring knife.

30   Put one side section of the mango into your palm and carefully begin to cut parallel lines with a small knife. The cuts should be approximately ½ an inch apart or closer. Watch out! Don't cut so deeply that you injure your palm. Rotate the mango half in your palm, and begin to make parallel cuts ½ an inch apart from each other. To insure that the mango cubes separate well, it is important that these cuts reach the peal all the way along. These cuts should form a grid.

31   Take the mango side in both of your hands, and turn it inside out. The mango cubes should stick out like the spikes on a porcupine, making it easy to gobble up the mango neatly. You may enjoy eating the scrumptious mango cubes right off the skin. You may also cut them off with a knife and serve them in a nice dish decorated with colorful pieces of other fruit.

32   Each pomegranate is filled with hundreds of sweet, juicy, edible ruby-red seeds. To keep these seeds intact, begin by using a small knife to make a long shallow cut right through the navel of the fruit. The cut should be no deeper

than the skin of the pomegranate. It should go halfway down both sides of the pomegranate. At the navel, make the cut slightly deeper than everywhere else. Next, make another cut perpendicular to the first. Both cuts should create a cross that divides the pomegranate into four sections. Place the blade of your knife into the gap of the cut and move it from side to side to open the pomegranate slightly. Repeat this move with the perpendicular cut.

33   Break the pomegranate into halves, and then quarters, with your hands.

34   After breaking the pomegranate into quarters, take the thin white peel off the seeds before you begin to eat them because this peel is quite bitter. The pits inside the seeds are edible.

35 Young coconuts, which contain about 750 ml of water, are healthiest to eat. As the coconut matures, the soft jelly inside hardens into flesh and loses some nutritional qualities. To choose a good coconut, pick one up and give it a shake. If it's a good one, it will be heavy and completely filled with liquid. Because it has no air bubbles, you won't be able to hear the water splash around inside. Of the many ways to open a coconut, we believe it's best to begin by setting the coconut on its side. The point (the top) should be pointing away from you. Take a large serrated knife and begin to shave the husk off of the point of the coconut so that the shell is revealed.

36 Rotate the coconut as needed and continue cutting off the husk all the way around the point. You will notice that under the white husk is a light brown shell. The coconuts usually seen in stores have their husk already removed. Make sure you have shaved off the husk in a complete circle so that it will be easier to open the coconut.

37 Place your knife just inside the circle you have shaved. Stab the knife into the shell. Coconut shells have a circular grain. When you force the knife through any part of the shell, a spherical crack will form. Cut about 1 inch into the shell of the coconut and slice down through the shell about 2 more inches. Put the coconut pointed side up again so that the coconut water does not run out. Twist the knife slightly and a round opening will easily form at the top of the coconut. When the coconut top is half way separated from the rest of the shell, you can use your hands to help lift the top off completely.

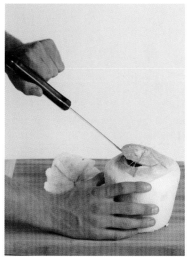

38 If you drink the water but don't want to eat the coconut meat right away, you may put the pointy shell top back on the coconut like a lid and store the coconut in the refrigerator for three or four days. To remove the coconut meat, use a spoon to scoop it out of the shell. The younger a coconut is, the thinner and softer the white meat will be. When the meat of a coconut is slightly pink, it means it is starting to ferment. In most cases, the coconut is still okay to eat, but both the meat and the water will taste different. If you have doubts, discard the coconut.

39　*Wild strawberries.* Found on mountain slopes and in forest settings, strawberries are shade-loving plants that grow in patches. See description,
page 181.

40　*Wild strawberry flowers.* The flowers of the wild strawberry are white. The
greens are best eaten when young and can be used in salads or smoothies.
The berries are delicious.

41   *Chickweed* is a common weed in gardens where the soil has been disturbed. It grows throughout the continental United States and prefers
moist, woodland areas. See description, page 182.

42   *Chickweed greens* are tender and mild. They can be eaten raw as a trailside
nibble or added into a salad.

43   *Clover.* Found in fields, lawns, and sunny meadows, and near roadways, both the flowers and leaves of clover can be eaten raw. Red clover makes a great decoration for salads, pâtés, pies, cakes, drinks, sandwiches, and anything else. See description, page 183.

44   *Dandelion.* Literally *dent de lion,* of "tooth of the lion" in French, dandelions have one yellow flower per stem. Greens can be used in salads, in smoothies, or as trailside nibbles. The flowers can be eaten raw or made into jam. And the roots can be eaten raw or dried and ground up for use as a coffee substitute. See description, page 184.

45   *Lamb's-quarter* can grow up to ten feet tall and is widespread throughout the United States. Lamb's-quarter can be eaten raw in salads, smoothies, and juices, or as a trailside nibble. The leaves resemble spinach in taste and texture. See description, page 184.

46   *Miner's lettuce.* The stem of miner's lettuce, which passes directly through the round leaf, is a key identifier of miner's lettuce. The whole plant can be eaten raw in salads or as a trail nibble. Miner's lettuce is very mild, tender, and, most of all, delicious. See description, page 186.

47   *Plantain* is commonly found in sunny meadows and near roadways. The tender leaves can be used as salad greens. The buds and flowers, which grow at the top of a long, narrow stem and bear slight resemblance to baby corn, can be marinated. See description, page 187.

48   *Purslane.* Hidden amid purslane leaves are tiny, yellow flowers. The whole purslane can be eaten raw and is both tasty and nutritious. It has a pleasant, slightly sour taste. It is a great source of omega-3 fatty acids, which prevent heart disease and improve immune system functions. See description, page 188.

49   *Sheep sorrel* likes disturbed soil and is found throughout the continental United States in empty fields, in rocky meadows, and along roadways. The tender leaves taste sour and make a lovely addition to smoothies or salad dressings. See description, page 189.

50   Both the leaves and flowers of sheep sorrel can be eaten raw in salads or as a trailside nibble. When crushed, added to water, and mixed with natural sweetener, sorrel leaves make a mouthwatering lemonade substitute when lemons are unavailable.

51 *Nettles.* Blending the stinging nettle plant destroys its needles and enables consumption in raw form. The same chemical compound the nettle plant produces that causes irritation actually soothes the skin. If you are stung by stinging nettles, apply fresh stinging nettle juice to the irritated area to completely neutralize the itch. See description, page 190.

52 *Thimbleberries* are red and closely resemble raspberries except that their overall shape is flatter. The berries are edible and very delicious, with a sweet and nutty taste. The flowers are also edible and make a delicious addition to salads. Thimbleberry leaves can be used either fresh or dried in herbal teas. See description, page 191.

PISTACHIO PARADISE

1   pound pistachio nuts (not soaked)
1   cup golden raisins
1   cup dried apples
2   tablespoons agave nectar
½   teaspoon nutmeg
⅕   teaspoon sea salt
    carob powder or coconut flakes to taste

Blend first 6 ingredients in food processor for 2 minutes or until thoroughly mixed. Take about a tablespoon of the mixture and roll it into a ball shape. Repeat process until blended mixture runs out. The balls can be rolled in shredded coconut or carob powder, or frozen to reduce surface stickiness. Yields 15 balls.

VERY SEEDY BARS

1   cup pumpkin seeds (not soaked)
1   cup sesame seeds (not soaked)
1   cup hemp seeds (not soaked)
1   cup poppy seeds (not soaked)
1   cup dried figs, chopped and soaked 15 minutes
½   cup golden raisins
1   teaspoon caramel extract
⅕   teaspoon sea salt
    carob powder or coconut flakes to taste

Blend first 8 ingredients in food processor for 2 minutes or until thoroughly mixed. Take about a tablespoon of the mixture and roll it into a ball shape. Repeat process until blended mixture runs out. The balls can be rolled in shredded coconut or carob powder, or frozen to reduce surface stickiness. Yields 15 balls.

PIÑA COLADA BARS

½   pound coconut flakes
½   pound macadamia nuts
1   cup dried pineapple, chopped and soaked 15
     minutes
½   cup golden raisins
1   teaspoon vanilla extract
⅕   teaspoon sea salt

Blend all ingredients in food processor in short bursts. The object is to mix all ingredients without pulverizing the food. Take about a handful of the mixture and use your hands to form it into a rectangular bar shape. Repeat process until blended mixture runs out. Place bars in freezer for 1 hour for better shape. This will also reduce surface stickiness. Yields 10 bars.

LEMON BARS

1   pound macadamia nuts (not soaked)
1   cup dried apples, soaked 15 minutes
1   cup dried golden mulberries
¼   cup lemon juice
1   tablespoon lemon zest
1   tablespoon honey
½   teaspoon lemon essential oil
⅕   teaspoon sea salt

Blend all ingredients in food processor in short bursts. The object is to mix all ingredients without pulverizing the food. Take about a handful of the mixture and use your hands to form it into a rectangular bar shape. Repeat process until blended mixture runs out. Place bars in freezer for 1 hour for better shape. This will also reduce surface stickiness. Yields 10 bars.

BRAZIL BLISS

1 pound Brazil nuts (not soaked)
1 cup dates, pitted
½ cup dried apricots
1 teaspoon caramel extract
1 teaspoon vanilla extract
⅕ teaspoon sea salt
  carob powder or coconut flakes to taste

Blend first 6 ingredients in food processor for 2 minutes or until thoroughly mixed. Take about a tablespoon of the mixture and roll it into a ball shape. Repeat process until blended mixture runs out. The balls can be rolled in shredded coconut or carob powder, or frozen to reduce surface stickiness. Yields 15 balls.

CASHEW CONFECTION

1 pound cashews (not soaked)
1½ cups dried mulberries
1 tablespoon vanilla extract
1 tablespoon carob powder
⅕ teaspoon sea salt
  coconut flakes or additional carob powder
  to taste

Blend first 5 ingredients in food processor for 2 minutes or until thoroughly mixed. Take about a tablespoon of mixture and roll it into a ball shape. Repeat process until blended mixture runs out. The balls can be rolled in shredded coconut or carob powder, or frozen to reduce surface stickiness. Yields 15 balls.

RICE CRISPY TREATS

2   cups buckwheat ground to flour in food
      processor (not presoaked)
1   cup ground sunflower seeds (not soaked)
½   cup agave nectar
½   teaspoon salt

Blend the buckwheat separately from the other ingredients. Then blend all remaining ingredients in a food processor and combine with buckwheat flour in a bowl. Knead this dough until uniformly mixed, and shape into squares. Dust with buckwheat flour. Serves 5.

cookies and scones

Thanks to the better food dehydrator models made available in the last decade, making raw cookies and scones has never been easier. We recommend using an Excalibur dehydrator, because its temperature is easily regulated and its design allows for constant airflow, which means that not only will the nutritional content of your recipe remain intact but also your cookies will have a unified consistency, making them more enjoyable to nibble on. For more information about the Excalibur, please refer to the "Meet Your New Appliances" section in Chapter One.

SUNRISE COOKIES

2   cups cashews
2   carrots, peeled and sliced
1   tablespoon vanilla

1	tablespoon raw honey
1/2	cup goji berries
1/2	teaspoon sea salt

Blend all ingredients in food processor for 1 minute or until thoroughly mixed. With an ice-cream scoop, scoop out dough onto dehydrator trays. Flatten dough to form desired cookie shapes. Dehydrate for 12–18 hours at 105°. Yields 7–8 cookies.

MANGO-ALMOND COOKIES

1	mango, peeled and chopped
1/2	cup almond pulp (from "Almond Milk" recipe on page 151)
2	tablespoons raw agave nectar

Blend all ingredients in food processor. Spread out onto dehydrator trays. Dry for 10–12 hours at 110°. Yields 8 cookies.

CHIA COOKIES

1	cup dried prunes, soaked in water 10 minutes
1	banana
1	pear
1/2	cup raw agave nectar
1/3	teaspoon sea salt
2	cups chia seeds, soaked 8 hours

Blend everything except soaked chia seeds in food processor. Mix chia seeds with liquified ingredients. Dehydrate for 12–18 hours at 105°. Yields 8 cookies.

PINE NUT THUMBPRINTS

1 cup pine nuts
¼ cup dates, pitted
1–1½ teaspoons raw agave nectar
1 teaspoon vanilla extract
1 pinch sea salt

Blend ingredients in food processor until fully mixed. Roll into medium-sized balls and use thumb to make an indentation for the filling.

FILLING

¼ cup fresh blueberries
1 teaspoon raw agave nectar
½ teaspoon cinnamon
  seasonal fruit

Blend first 3 filling ingredients in a blender until smooth. Pour mixture into thumbprints. Garnish with seasonal fruit. Fairchild mandarins are a wonderful addition. Serves 5.

CASHEW-ORANGE THUMBPRINTS

2 cups cashews
¼ cup dried apples
¼ cup dried figs
¼ cup dried apricots

Blend ingredients in food processor for 1 minute. If necessary, add water or apple juice to help blend. Roll into medium-sized balls and use thumb to make an indentation for the filling.

1	fresh mango, peeled and chopped
½	cup dried apples
½	teaspoon vanilla extract
¼	cup water

Blend ingredients in blender for 2 minutes or until smooth. Spoon mixture into thumbprints. Serves 5. See plate 19.

cereaL anD GranoLa

Eating raw cereal and granola for breakfast is something to look forward to when you wake up in the morning. The crispy fresh recipes found in this section are perfect for eating with any nut or seed milk. Because all the ingredients are whole and fresh, your cereal will maintain a pleasant consistency and never get mushy. Because of their long shelf life, compact size, and relatively low weight, cereal and granola prepared for a road or backpacking trip will make the trip more enjoyable and delicious.

CUP-O-BUCKWHEAT

2	cups buckwheat, soaked and sprouted 24 hours
½	cup dates, pitted and chopped
¼	cup raisins
1	teaspoon cinnamon
¼	cup raw honey

Mix ingredients in a bowl. Spread onto dehydrator trays and dry for 10–12 hours at 110°. Eat the cereal plain as a snack or with almond milk for breakfast. Serves 3.

SIMPLE PLEASURE

½   pound almonds, soaked overnight
½   pound rolled oats, soaked 15 minutes
1   cup dates, pitted
2   tablespoons honey
1   tablespoon vanilla extract

Blend all ingredients in food processor in short bursts. The object is to mix all ingredients without pulverizing them. Spread the mixture on dehydrator trays and dry for 10–14 hours at 110°. Enjoy with almond milk and fresh fruit, or eat plain as an on-the-go snack. Yields 1 pound of granola.

WALNUT-CRANBERRY BLISS

½   pound walnuts, soaked overnight
½   pound pumpkin seeds, soaked overnight
1   cup rolled rye flakes, soaked 15 minutes
1   cup dried cranberries
2–3 tablespoons agave nectar
1   teaspoon cinnamon powder
¼   teaspoon sea salt

Blend all ingredients in food processor in short bursts. The object is to mix all ingredients without pulverizing them! Spread the mixture on dehydrator trays and dry for 10–14 hours at 110°. Enjoy with almond milk and fresh fruit, or eat plain as an on-the-go snack. Yields 1 pound of granola.

SUNRISE CEREAL

½   pound almonds, soaked overnight
½   pound macadamia nuts, soaked overnight
½   pound cashews, soaked overnight
1   cup golden raisins
½   cup dried persimmons, chopped into ¼-inch pieces
½   cup dried cherries
2   tablespoons organic date sugar or agave nectar
2   pinches fresh lemon zest

Blend all ingredients in food processor in short bursts. The object is to mix all ingredients without pulverizing the food. Spread the mixture on dehydrator trays and dry for 10–14 hours at 110°. Enjoy with almond milk and fresh fruit, or eat plain as an on-the-go snack. Yields 1½ pounds of granola.

DATE WITH A STRAWBERRY GRANOLA

½   pound hazelnuts, soaked overnight
½   pound rolled oats, soaked 15 minutes
1   cup buckwheat, soaked overnight
1   cup dried strawberries
¼   cup dates, pitted
2   tablespoons honey
1   tablespoon carob powder
¼   teaspoon sea salt

Blend all ingredients in food processor in short bursts. The object is to mix all ingredients without pulverizing the food. Spread the mixture on dehydrator trays and dry for 10–14 hours at 110°. Enjoy with almond milk and fresh-cut strawberries. Yields 1 pound of granola.

PISTACHIO CRUNCH

½   pound shelled pistachios, soaked overnight
½   pound buckwheat, soaked overnight
½   pound almonds, soaked overnight
1   cup coconut flakes
1   cup dried mulberries
¼   cup dried apples, chopped
2   tablespoons honey
1   teaspoon powdered nutmeg
1   teaspoon powdered cinnamon
¼   teaspoon sea salt

Blend all ingredients in food processor in short bursts. The object is to mix all ingredients without pulverizing the food. Spread the mixture on dehydrator trays and dry for 10–14 hours at 110°. Enjoy with almond milk and fresh fruit, or eat plain as an on-the-go snack. Yields 1½ pounds of granola.

SPICY TROPICAL TRADE WIND

½   pound macadamia nuts, soaked overnight
½   pound almonds, soaked overnight
¼   pound pecans, soaked overnight
1   cup coconut flakes
½   cup golden raisins
½   cup dried mango, chopped into ¼-inch pieces
½   lime, juiced
½   teaspoon powdered cayenne pepper
2   tablespoons honey
2   pinches lime zest

Blend all ingredients in food processor in short bursts. The object is to mix all ingredients without pulverizing the food! Spread the mixture on dehydrator trays and dry for 10–14 hours at 110°. Enjoy with almond milk and fresh fruit, or eat plain as an on-the-go snack. Yields 1½ pounds of granola.

HEMPY O'S

½	pound almonds, soaked overnight
½	pound walnuts, soaked overnight
½	pound rolled oats, soaked 15 minutes
1	cup hemp seeds
1	cup dates, pitted
2	tablespoons agave nectar
1	tablespoon vanilla extract
¼	teaspoon sea salt

Blend all ingredients in food processor in short bursts. The object is to mix all ingredients without pulverizing the food. Spread the mixture on dehydrator trays and dry for 10–14 hours at 110°. Enjoy with almond milk and fresh fruit, or eat plain as an on-the-go snack. Yields 1 pound of granola.

PEANUT CRUNCH

½	pound peanuts, soaked overnight
½	pound rolled oats, soaked 15 minutes
¼	pound almonds, soaked overnight
1	cup dates, pitted
½	cup coconut flakes
2	tablespoons honey
1	teaspoon vanilla extract
1	teaspoon sea salt

Blend all ingredients in food processor in short bursts. The object is to mix all ingredients without pulverizing the food. Spread the mixture on dehydrator trays and dry for 10–14 hours at 110°. Enjoy with almond milk and fresh fruit, or eat plain as an on-the-go snack. Yields 1 pound of granola.

OATMEAL CEREAL

2   cups rolled oats, soaked 15 minutes
½   cup dates, pitted
1–1½ cups water
2   tablespoons honey
1   tablespoon vanilla extract
1   tablespoon coconut oil
¼   teaspoon honey
     seasonal fruit, citrus zest, mint to taste

Blend first 7 ingredients in blender for 2 minutes or until creamy. Mix with seasonal fruit. Garnish with lemon or lime zest and mint before serving. Serves 2–3.

BARLEY BREAKFAST

1   cup barley, soaked overnight
1   cup almond milk
½   cup fresh blueberries
½   cup fresh raspberries
5   tablespoons agave nectar

Mix all ingredients in a bowl and serve. Serves 3.

Jams, Puddings, and Yogurts

Making raw jams is a valuable way to maintain variety and excitement in your diet if you reside in a cold climate. For example, our relatives in Russia do not have access to many fruits during the wintertime. They use the fruits from summer and preserve them so that they can be enjoyed at a later time. The conventional way to make jam requires some heavy processing, which takes nutrients out of the food. This lack of nutrients is unfortunate, because your body needs more of them during the winter months. The good news is that jams can easily be made raw! By blending fresh fruits with dried ones, you can preserve your creation for months using the naturally occurring sugars. This means that you can make jam in the fall that will nourish your body until spring, when there are fresh fruits and veggies to munch on.

There is nothing easier to make than a scrumptious raw pudding or a cultured yogurt. As you will find out later in this section, by simply blending a ripe mango and nothing else, your taste buds can be immersed in one of the most heavenly flavors they've ever been exposed to. We invite you to add to our original recipes, alter them, and create your own amazing puddings.

RAW MANGO JAM

This recipe may be used for making jam out of any other dried fruit. Simply replace the dried mango with another dried fruit. The quality of the dried fruit you use is important. We prefer to use fruit that we ourselves have dried during the harvest season, but often we can find quality dried fruit from health food stores.

2   cups dried mangoes, presoaked in water 10 minutes
⅓   cup water

Blend until smooth. Serves 5.

BLUEBERRY JAM

2   cups dried blueberries
⅓   cup water

Blend until smooth. Serves 5.

PEAR JAM

2   cups dried pears, presoaked in water 10 minutes

⅓   cup water

Blend until smooth. Serves 5.

STRAWBERRY JAM

2   cups dried strawberries, presoaked in water 10 minutes

⅓   cup water

Blend until smooth. Serves 5.

PERSIMMON JAM

2   cups dried persimmons, presoaked in water 10 minutes

⅓   cup water

Blend until smooth. Serves 5.

ORANGE PUDDING

1   young coconut (meat and water)

1   fresh mango, peeled and pitted

½   cup dried mango, presoaked in water 10 minutes

6   dates, pitted

½   teaspoon orange extract

mint to taste

Pour coconut water into the blender. Add coconut meat and the next 4 ingredients. Blend for 2 minutes or until creamy and smooth. If necessary, add water to help with blending dried fruit. Serve with a sprig of mint in each glass. Serves 2–3.

YOUNG COCONUT YOGURT

9   young coconuts (meat only)
4   quarts young coconut water
1   packet yogurt culture mix*

Blend coconut meat together with coconut water and yogurt culture packet in the blender for 3 minutes or until smooth. Pour mixture into a gallon jar and stir vigorously for 2–3 minutes. Cover the jar with cloth and let stand on counter for 1–2 days at room temperature. Once yogurt has become thick and slightly fermented, store in the refrigerator. Yields 1 gallon.

DELICIOUS PUDDING

1   white nectarine
1   cup blackberries
1   cup dried mango, soaked in water 15 minutes

Blend in blender and enjoy. Serves 2.

*Yogurt culture packets can be purchased in most health-food stores. Of course, the dairy-free cultures are the best. Culture packets are expensive; however, keep in mind that 1 packet can potentially make infinite batches of yogurt. Just save 1 cup of your yogurt and use it in place of the culture packet the next time you make coconut yogurt.

EZ MANGO PUDDING

1   mango, peeled and chopped

Blend in blender. Serves 1.

EZ MANGO PUDDING 2

1   mango, peeled and chopped
½   lime, juiced
5   dates, pitted

Blend ingredients in blender. Enjoy! Serves 1.

SILLY MANGO PUDDING

1   mango, peeled
1   orange
1   pear
1   banana
2   cups water
3   tablespoons psyllium husk powder

Blend the fruit, and then add the psyllium husk powder. After blending, quickly pour blender contents into glasses because the pudding will set within a matter of minutes. Serves 4.

CASHEW PUDDING

⅓   cup cashews
1   mango
1   teaspoon honey

5   mint leaves
½   cup water

Blend thoroughly. Serves 3.

FLUFFY VANILLA PUDDING

1   cup almond milk
2   ripe bananas
6   dates
½   teaspoon vanilla
⅕   teaspoon nutmeg

Blend in blender. Serves 2–3.

STRAWBERRY-COCONUT PUDDING

1   coconut (meat only)
½   cup coconut water
1   basket strawberries
1   tablespoon agave nectar

Blend in blender. Serves 2–3. See plate 18.

STRAWBERRY PUDDING

1   basket fresh strawberries
1   avocado
1   teaspoon honey
¼   cup orange juice

Blend in blender. Serves 2–3.

WALNUT-DATE PUDDING

1   cup orange juice
1   cup dates, pitted
⅓   cup walnuts
½   teaspoon vanilla

Blend in blender. Serves 2–3.

GREEN PUDDING

1   large avocado
6   dates
⅕   teaspoon salt

Blend in Blender. Serves 2–3.

FOUR

❧ Drinks

Green Smoothies

Are you too busy to prepare healthful food? No problem! Here is your solution: when Sergei was in college, he needed every spare moment of time for his studies. He didn't have time to prepare fancy dishes but at the same time did not want to give up his source of good health by eating fast food. Every morning before leaving for school, he blended any greens that he had on hand with any available fruit. This only took moments, because blending only required the flip of a switch and cleanup, consisting of holding the blender container under a stream of running water. Sergei showed up to class with a glass jar of green smoothie every day. This kept him going strong; nourished his body with protein, chlorophyll, vitamins, and minerals; and kept his brain functioning properly. Furthermore, because of their dense nutrition and high fiber content, green smoothies kept Sergei's hunger at bay until the evening, when he had enough time to eat a solid meal.

❧❧❧

GREEN SMOOTHIE OF WONDER

3	generous handfuls spinach
3	peaches
2	cups apple juice
1	mango

Blend in blender until smooth. Serves 3–4.

BLUE-GREEN ALOE SMOOTHIE

2	cups water
1	head romaine lettuce
1	medium Fuji apple
¼	lime
¼	cup blueberries (fresh or frozen)
1	small leaf aloe

Blend all ingredients in blender for 2 minutes or until smooth. Pour into glasses and enjoy. Note: this is a great drink for diabetics, because blueberries and aloe naturally reduce blood sugar. Serves 2–3.

GREEN TANGERINE

½	head green leaf lettuce
5	tangerines (seeds removed to avoid bitterness)
1	banana

Blend all ingredients in blender for 2 minutes or until smooth. Pour into glasses and enjoy! Serves 1–2.

GREEN-O-LICIOUS

2   handfuls spinach
2   cups orange juice
1   grapefruit (seeds removed to avoid bitterness)
1   mango

Blend all ingredients in blender for 2 minutes or until smooth. Pour into glasses and enjoy! Serves 2.

COOL DAY

½   bunch romaine lettuce
1   frozen banana, peeled
½   bag red or green seedless grapes
1   basket strawberries

Blend all ingredients in blender for 2 minutes or until smooth. Serve 1–2.

SPINACH-APPLE SMOOTHIE

2   cups water
2   cups spinach
1   medium mango, peeled and chopped
1   quince
1   medium Fuji apple
1   medium banana
1   orange, sliced

Blend first 6 ingredients in blender for 1 minute or until smooth. Serve with orange slices. Serves 2–3.

GREEN AH-HA!
EPIPHANY SMOOTHIE

1 head butter lettuce
1 mango
¼ medium watermelon (rind removed)

Blend ingredients in blender for 1 minute or until smooth. Serves 2–3.

BERRY BAZOOKA BLAST

1 pint fresh strawberries
1 pint fresh raspberries
1 head romaine lettuce
1 succulent peach
1 cup water

Blend all ingredients in blender for 2 minutes or until smooth. Pour into glasses and enjoy! Serves 2–3.

GREEN SMOOTHIE NUMBER 1156

2 cups water
½ bunch dinosaur kale
1 large pear, chopped with core
¼ cup cranberries
1 medium mango, peeled and chopped
½ apple

Blend ingredients in blender for 1 minute or until smooth. Garnish and serve. Serves 2–3.

GREEN GOODNESS

2	cups water
1	head romaine lettuce
1	bunch parsley
½	small pineapple
1	banana
1	pear

Blend in a blender until smooth. Serves 2.

GENERIC GREEN SMOOTHIE

2	cups water
½	bunch curly kale
2	medium apples
1	banana

Blend in blender until smooth. Serves 2.

smoothies and shakes

Fruit smoothies are a perfect treat on a hot summer day. Summertime is a time of abundance, nourishment, and heat! We have noticed that when the temperature is hot outside, eating a heavy entrée or vegetable salad topped with dressing can be quite unappetizing. On the other hand, fruits are cleansing and digest quicker than veggies. Naturally our bodies are drawn to this option, because we can receive necessary nutrients to stay healthy and calories for energy without the side effects of feeling heavy. Blending a cool, refreshing fruit smoothie on a hot summer day takes staying light to another plane, because the blending process ruptures the food on a cellular level, making it even easier for the body to digest.

GREAT SMOOTHIE OF GOODNESS

1 small pineapple, peeled, cored, and chopped
1 large mango, peeled, cored, and chopped
1 half-pinkie-sized piece fresh ginger
3–4 ice cubes

Blend all ingredients in blender. Pour into fancy glass and garnish with mint and thin orange slices. Serves 2–3.

SERGEI'S FAVORITE SMOOTHIE

2 oranges, peeled
2 frozen bananas (or substitute other frozen fruits)

Blend ingredients in blender until smooth. Place the oranges toward the bottom of blender to make enough liquid to blend the frozen bananas. Garnish with fresh strawberries. Serves 2.

CHOCOLATE MILK SHAKE

1 young coconut (meat and water)
¼ cup pine nuts
5–6 dates, pitted
1 heaping tablespoon carob powder
1 teaspoon vanilla extract
1 pinch sea salt

Blend all ingredients in blender. Pour into fancy glass and garnish with mint or lemon balm. Serves 2.

DEEP BLUE
(WITH A LITTLE PURPLE)

2   frozen bananas
1   pint fresh, ripe blueberries
1   cup orange juice

Blend all ingredients in blender until smooth. Serves 2–3.

DURIAN MANIA

Durian is an exotic spiky fruit from Thailand.

½   cup durian meat
½   cup young coconut meat
¼   dates, pitted
    cups coconut water
1   teaspoon vanilla extract

Blend all ingredients in blender until smooth. Serves 2–3.

BANANGO SMOOTHIE

You can make great parfait with this smoothie.

2   frozen bananas
1½   cups frozen mango chunks
1   cup orange juice

Blend all ingredients in blender until smooth. Serves 2–3.

ALMOND MILK SHAKE

3	cups almond milk
½	cup fresh or frozen strawberries
1	medium orange, peeled and chopped
1	fresh or frozen banana
¼	cup dates, pitted
½	teaspoon sea salt
1	teaspoon vanilla extract
½	cup ice

Blend all ingredients in blender until smooth. Garnish with fruit before serving. Serves 3–4.

OUR FIRST SMOOTHIE

This smoothie tastes good every time and has impressed many people.

2	frozen bananas
½	large avocado
1	pint strawberries
1	cup water

Blend all ingredients in blender until smooth. Serves 2–3.

CHOCOLATE BLIZZARD

1	cup almond milk
2–3	frozen bananas
5–8	dates, pitted

1–2 tablespoons raw carob
1 whole vanilla bean

Blend all ingredients in blender until smooth. Garnish with orange slices before serving. Serves 2–3.

COOL SUMMER SHAKE

2 cups almond milk (see "Almond Milk" recipe on page 151)
½ cup pomegranate seeds
¼ cup rosewater
4–6 ice cubes
1 banana

Blend all ingredients in blender for 2 minutes or until smooth. Garnish with orange slices or seasonal fruit prior to serving. Serves 2–3.

PERSIMMON NIGHTS

2 cups almond milk (see "Almond Milk" recipe on page 151)
2 persimmons, pitted
3–4 dates, pitted
1 tablespoon vanilla extract

Blend all ingredients in blender for 2 minutes or until smooth. Dust with powdered cinnamon or nutmeg. Serves 2–3.

GREEN BANANGO BLISS

1	ripe mango, pitted, peeled, and chopped
1	ripe banana
1	cup freshly made apple juice
4–6	ice cubes
1–2	tablespoons spirulina

Blend all ingredients in blender for 2 minutes or until smooth. Garnish with fresh-cut strawberries. Serves 2.

STRAWBERRY GOLDEN KIWI SHAKE

2	cups Brazil nut milk (see "Brazil Coconut Milk" recipe on page 134)
1	pint fresh strawberries
2–3	golden kiwis, peeled
4–5	dates, pitted
1	ripe banana
4–6	ice cubes

Blend all ingredients in blender for 2 minutes or until smooth. Garnish with fresh-cut seasonal fruit. Serves 2–3.

MIDNIGHT MADNESS

2–3	cups hazelnut milk (see "Silky Hazelnut Milky" recipe on page 133)
5–8	dates, pitted
2	tablespoons raw carob powder
1	tablespoon vanilla extract
¼	teaspoon salt

¼   teaspoon cayenne
¼   teaspoon powdered nutmeg
4–6 ice cubes

Blend all ingredients in blender for 2 minutes or until smooth.
Sprinkle with cocoa nibs before serving. Serves 2–3.

MANGO-MINT LIME

2   ripe mangoes, pitted, peeled, and chopped
1   cup water
½   lime, juiced
3–4 sprigs mint
3–4 ice cubes

Blend all ingredients in blender for 2 minutes or until smooth.
Garnish with fresh mint leaves before serving. Serves 2.

TROPICAL SWIRL

2   cups almond milk (see "Almond Milk" recipe
    on page 129)
1   strawberry papaya, peeled, pitted, and
    chopped
1   pint fresh strawberries
1   ripe banana
1   cup pineapple, peeled and chopped
4–5 ice cubes

Blend all ingredients in blender for 2 minutes or until smooth.
Garnish with fresh mint leaves before serving. Serves 2.

DATE WITH A COCONUT

1   young coconut (meat and water and water)
3–4 dates, pitted
1   teaspoon vanilla extract

Blend all ingredients in blender for 2 minutes or until smooth.
Serves 1. See plate 18.

BLUEBERRY BLISS

1   young coconut (meat and water)
3–4 dates, pitted
1   pint fresh blueberries
1   banana
3–4 ice cubes

Blend all ingredients in blender for 2 minutes or until smooth.
Serves 1–2.

NUTTIN RHYMES
WITH "ORANGE" SHAKE

2   cups almond milk (see "Almond Milk" recipe
      on page 151)
4–5 dates, pitted
1   ripe banana
1   tablespoon orange extract
1   teaspoon vanilla extract
½   lemon, juiced

Blend all ingredients in blender for 2 minutes or until smooth.
Serves 2.

juices

When transitioning to a raw-food diet, you may feel sad to part with the wide array of drinks that you no longer choose to sip. Lucky for you, raw juices are not only easy to make but also easy to drink because they taste quite delicious. Your friends will be green with jealousy when they see you drinking a frothy pineapple juice instead of a carbonated, sugar-filled soda pop. As soon as you try the authentic taste of any fresh juice, you will realize instantly how bad commercial soft-drink makers are at recreating a natural flavor. Of all the things we initially craved when we switched our diets, bottled juices and drinks were not on our list. Fresh juices enrich any meal, be it raw or cooked.

ANNA'S EXCEPTIONAL JUICE

5	pears
3	carrots
1	apple

Juice together in a juicer and enjoy. Serves 3.

WATERMELON WOW JUICE

½	medium watermelon, peeled
2	lemons, peeled with seeds removed
2	inches fresh ginger
4	apples

Juice all ingredients together in a juicer and enjoy. Serves 6.

VEGGIE DELIGHT

3	medium tomatoes
2	stalks celery
1	red bell pepper
1	lemon
1	cucumber
⅓	bunch cilantro
2	cloves garlic

Juice all ingredients in a juicer and enjoy. Serves 3.

RAW FAMILY'S GREEN JUICE

1	large bunch kale, chopped
2	medium apples, chopped
½	lemon with peel, chopped
1	cup water

Blend all ingredients well in blender for 1 minute. Strain the liquid through a nut-milk bag or strainer. Serves 3–4.

FANCY DELICIOUS JUICE

1	cantaloupe
1	pint fresh blueberries

Juice all ingredients together in a juicer and enjoy! Serves 2.

JOINT LUBRICATOR

1	bunch celery
2	cucumbers
1	apple (for mild sweetening)

Juice through a juicer and enjoy while fresh. Serves 1–2.

GINGERSNAP JUICE

8–10 apples
1   large piece ginger

Juice through juicer. Enjoy! Serves 3–5.

KALE-IDOSCOPE

1   bunch dinosaur kale
5   pears
1   lemon with peel

Juice through juicer. Serves 1–2.

TOMATO MANIA

8–10 large tomatoes
½   bunch celery
4–5 cloves garlic

Juice through juicer. Serves 2–4.

BROOK'S WINE

2   peeled beets
5–8 apples
1   lemon with peel

Juice through juicer. Serves 1–2.

sun teas and coolers

As exciting as juices can be, we sometimes succumb to laziness, because the idea of assembling, using, and cleaning a juicer makes us cringe. If you can relate to this feeling, here's a bountiful array of juicer-free drink recipes. With a gallon glass jar, some water, and a few other easy-to-find ingredients, you'll be well on your way to sipping a sensational, succulent drinks from the comfort of your couch!

LEMONADE

½   lemon, juiced
8   ounces water
1   tablespoon agave nectar or honey

Add the agave and lemon into a glass. Pour in water and stir. Serves 1.

SUN TEA

This is a great drink on a hot summer day. Sergei likes to drink Sun Tea after running. Sun Tea is a good substitute for black and green teas or coffee.

½   bunch peppermint
½   bunch spearmint

Place in a gallon jar and fill with water. Let soak in sun for 8 hours, then enjoy with ice. Yields 1 gallon.

MINT AID

1   quart water
⅓   cup Meyer lemon juice

5   sprigs fresh mint
1½   tablespoons raw honey (manuka honey
     preferred)

Juice lemons and mix thoroughly with honey. You may need to
blend lemon juice and honey in a blender to get the honey to
dissolve. Add mint and transfer into a quart jar. Add enough water
to fill the jar. Mix again by shaking. Chill and serve. Note: this
recipe also makes a nice winter drink if the water is heated slightly.
Serves 1–2.

LEMONY MINT SUN TEA

1–2 bunches fresh mint
1   lemon, sliced with skin
4   tablespoons honey

Place all ingredients in a glass gallon jar. Fill jar with water. Mix
ingredients thoroughly with a spoon or ladle. Cover the top of jar
with a lid and place in sunlight for 12 hours. Serve chilled or with
ice cubes. Yields 1 gallon.

PEACH COOLER

1   cup dried peaches, chopped
½   cup dried hibiscus tea
1   fresh bunch lemon balm
4–5 tablespoons honey

Place all ingredients in a glass gallon jar. Fill jar with water. Mix
ingredients thoroughly with a spoon or ladle. Cover the top of jar
with a lid and place in sunlight for 12 hours. Serve chilled or with
ice cubes. Yields 1 gallon.

PINE-NEEDLE TEA

1–2 cups freshly harvested pine needles, chopped
into ½-inch pieces
1 lemon, sliced with skin
4–5 tablespoons honey

Place all ingredients in a glass gallon jar. Fill jar with water. Mix ingredients thoroughly with a spoon or ladle. Cover the top of jar with a lid and place in sunlight for 12 hours. Serve chilled or with ice cubes. Yields 1 gallon.

ROSE-MINT WATER

1–2 cups freshly picked rose petals
½ bunch fresh mint

Place all ingredients in a glass gallon jar. Fill jar with water. Mix ingredients thoroughly with a spoon or ladle. Cover the top of jar with a lid and place in sunlight for 12 hours. Serve chilled or with ice cubes. Sweeten with honey if desired. Yields 1 gallon.

OREGANO WATER

1 bunch fresh oregano
1 lemon, sliced with skin
4 tablespoons honey

Place all ingredients in a glass gallon jar. Fill jar with water. Mix ingredients thoroughly with a spoon or ladle. Cover the top of jar with a lid and place in sunlight for 12 hours. Serve chilled or with ice cubes. Yields 1 gallon.

SPICY CHILE LIME

3   cups apple cider
1   lime, sliced with peel
3   tablespoons honey
1   teaspoon chile powder
½   cup dried orange peels

Place all ingredients in a glass gallon jar. Fill jar with water. Mix ingredients thoroughly with a spoon or ladle. Cover the top of jar with a lid and place in sunlight for 12 hours. Serve chilled or with ice cubes. Yields 1 gallon.

JAS-MINT WATER

½   cup jasmine flowers
½   bunch fresh spearmint
4   tablespoons honey

Place all ingredients in a glass gallon jar. Fill jar with water. Mix ingredients thoroughly with a spoon or ladle. Cover the top of jar with a lid and place in sunlight for 12 hours. Serve chilled or with ice cubes. Yields 1 gallon.

CALM TEA

½   cup rose hips
¼   cup chamomile
¼   cup raspberry leaves
¼   cup juniper berries
¼   cup dried orange peels

Place all ingredients in a glass gallon jar. Fill jar with water. Mix ingredients thoroughly with a spoon or ladle. Cover the top of jar with a lid and place in sunlight for 12 hours. Serve chilled or with ice cubes. Yields 1 gallon.

CINNA-MINT WATER

4–5 cinnamon sticks
½ bunch fresh mint
¼ cup dried lemon peel

Place all ingredients in a glass gallon jar. Fill jar with water. Mix ingredients thoroughly with a spoon or ladle. Cover the top of jar with a lid and place in sunlight for 12 hours. Serve chilled or with ice cubes. Yields 1 gallon.

HIBISCUS COOLER

¼ cup dried hibiscus flowers, soaked in warm or hot water
4 cups warm or hot water
2–3 tablespoons honey
1 pinkie-sized piece ginger, peeled and sliced into thin rounds
¼ lemon

Soak hibiscus flowers for 15–20 minutes or until water turns bright red. Strain flowers away from water. Mix content with honey and ginger. Add warm or hot water to the mix to dilute. Slice lemon with skin into thin rounds. Serve drink with floating lemon rounds. This is an elegant drink, appropriate for any event or social gathering. Note: if the ginger is sliced thinly, you do not need to strain it away prior to serving. Serves 4–5.

NUT and seed MILKS

When we were transitioning to a raw diet, nut and seed milks were not yet commercially available. Because we needed a milk substitute for cereal, shakes, and other specialty drinks, we had to create milk from nuts. For this section we present a whole fleet of nut and seed milks, which we feel rival not only dairy milk but also the nut and seed milks now available nationwide at any supermarket. It is important to note that the process of making milk involves straining away the liquid portion from the solid; while the recipes instruct how to make milk (the liquid), one should not dispose of the pulp (the solid), because it can be used in other recipes such as for pâtés, cookies, cakes, and pies. Many of the milks themselves can also be used in other recipes, such as those for shakes, smoothies, and frozen desserts.

ALMOND MILK

3   cups almonds, soaked overnight
8   cups distilled water
5   dates or 2 tablespoons raw honey
1   teaspoon sea salt

Drain water from the almonds. Blend almonds and water in the blender for 3 minutes or until smooth. Strain the mixture until almond pulp is dry enough to stick together. Pour strained milk back into the blender and blend with salt and dates. Enjoy! Note: if you like your milk to be richer, use less water. If you prefer skim milk, use more water. Serves 5–7.

SILKY MILK

2   cups almond milk
1   banana
⅓   teaspoon pumpkin pie spice

Blend thoroughly. Serves 3.

CHAI

2	cups almonds, soaked overnight
6	cups water
1	teaspoon honey
1	teaspoon clove
1	teaspoon nutmeg
½	teaspoon cinnamon
½	teaspoon sea salt

Blend almonds and water in the blender for 3 minutes or until smooth. Strain mixture. Pour liquid back into blender and mix the remaining ingredients. Serves 6–7.

CHOCOLATE ALMOND MILK

This is a great dessert.

1	quart almond milk
½	cup dates
1	young coconut (meat and water)
2	tablespoons raw carob powder
1	raw vanilla bean

Blend well in a blender. Serve chilled. Serves 2–3.

GENERIC NUT MILK

2	cups any nuts, soaked overnight
5–6	cups water (depending on desired richness)

Blend all ingredients in food processor for 1 minute or until smooth. Strain mixture through nut-milk bag or strainer. Yields 7 cups.

SILKY HAZELNUT MILKY

2 cups hazelnuts, soaked overnight
5 cups water
½ cup dates, pitted
1 teaspoon vanilla extract
⅕ teaspoon sea salt

Blend all ingredients in blender for 1 minute or until smooth. Strain mixture through nut-milk bag or strainer. Chill before serving. Yields 7 cups.

MACADAMIA NUT MILK

2 cups macadamia nuts, soaked overnight
5–6 cups water
2 tablespoons honey
1 teaspoon cinnamon
⅕ teaspoon sea salt

Blend all ingredients in blender for 1 minute or until smooth. Strain mixture through nut-milk bag or strainer. Chill before serving. Yields 7 cups.

SESAME MILK

2 cups sesame seeds, soaked overnight
4–5 cups water
6–8 dates, pitted
1 tablespoon honey
⅕ teaspoon sea salt

Blend all ingredients in blender for 1 minute or until smooth. Strain mixture through nut-milk bag or strainer. Chill before serving. Yields 5 cups.

BRAZIL COCONUT MILK

2   cups Brazil nuts, soaked overnight
1   cup coconut flakes
6–7 cups water
5–7 dates, pitted
1   teaspoon vanilla extract
1/5 teaspoon sea salt

Blend all ingredients in blender for 1 minute or until smooth. Strain mixture through nut-milk bag or strainer. Chill before serving. Yields 7 cups.

CASHEW MILK

2   cups cashews, soaked overnight
5–6 cups water
2   tablespoon honey
1/5 teaspoon sea salt

Blend all ingredients in blender for 1 minute or until smooth. Strain mixture through nut-milk bag or strainer. Chill before serving. Yields 7 cups.

HEMP SEED MILK

1 1/2 cups hemp seeds, soaked 2 hours
1/2   cup sesame seeds, soaked 2 hours
5   cups water
5–7   dates, pitted
1/5   teaspoon sea salt

Blend all ingredients in blender for 1 minute or until smooth. Strain mixture through nut-milk bag or strainer. Chill before serving. Yields 6 cups.

PUMPKIN SEED MILK

2   cups pumpkin seeds, soaked overnight
5   cups water
½   cup raisins
2   tablespoons agave nectar
1   teaspoon powdered nutmeg
⅕   teaspoon sea salt

Blend all ingredients in blender for 1 minute or until smooth. Strain mixture through nut-milk bag or strainer. Chill before serving. Yields 6 cups.

FIVE

Marinated and Fermented Foods

Incorporating fermented foods into our diet brings with it many wonderful benefits. The process of fermentation produces a healthful bacteria known as *acidophilus*. Among some of the benefits of acidophilus are good colon and intestinal health, proper digestion of food, and healthy bowel movements.[1] It is no wonder that all ancient cultures ate some form of fermented foods, ranging from sauerkraut in Europe, kimchi in Asia, and yogurt and kefir worldwide. By using the recipes in this chapter, you will learn how easy it is to make acidophilus-rich foods.

Learning how to make marinated dishes will bring elegance and style to your career as a raw-food chef. Whether you choose to pursue cooking professionally or merely showing off your skills to family and friends, marinated foods definitely get mouths watering. After you see what is required to create a marinated concoction, we dare you to come up with your own recipes. Note: to ensure that your kimchi will be cultured with good bacteria, we recommend using a high-quality brand of kefir culture from a nondairy source.

᚛᚛᚛

SAUERKRAUT

3 medium heads cabbage
5 carrots
4 cups distilled water
2 tablespoons sea salt
1 tablespoon dill seed
8 bay leaves

Grate cabbage and carrots into a large bowl or crock. Save half a head of cabbage to add into the blender. Blend cabbage, water, and salt in the blender for 1 minute. Pour liquid into the grated ingredients, and then add the dill seed and bay leaves. Mix all ingredients vigorously for 3 minutes. Cover the mixture with a plate and something heavy, such as a container of water, to keep the juice coming up. Don't let cabbage dry out on top. Yields 1½ gallons. See plate 10.

SPICY KIMCHI

1 large head Napa cabbage, chopped into 1-inch pieces
3 large carrots, peeled and grated
1 bunch green onions, sliced
1 thumb-sized piece ginger, diced
2–3 cloves garlic, minced
½ small habañero pepper, diced
1–2 teaspoons sea salt

Place cabbage, carrots, and green onions in a glass bowl or jar. Add remaining ingredients and mix until enough liquids are produced to keep food fully submerged. The salt should help draw out cabbage juices, but it may be necessary to add a little water to submerge jar content completely. To further aid this process, blend salt, habañero, and ginger with a little water and some cabbage. Pour mixture over jar content and cover with breathable lid or cloth. Allow jar content to sit at room temperature for 2–3 days. After 2–3 days, place jar in refrigerator to stop fermentation process. Lightly drizzle with olive oil or serve plain. *Note:* ingredients not submerged in liquid will decompose instead of ferment! Yields ¾ gallon.

PICKLED ZUCCHINI AND EGGPLANT

People who dislike the taste of plain, raw zucchini or eggplant will rave over this dish.

Chop the following ingredients and place in a gallon jar:

1	eggplant
3–4	medium green zucchini
3–4	yellow zucchini

Blend the following ingredients in a blender:

1	cup water
6–8	cloves garlic
1	tablespoon sea salt
2	tablespoons honey
¼	bunch fresh oregano
¼	bunch fresh thyme
¼	cup apple cider vinegar

Pour blended mixture into jar over sliced veggies. Using your hands, work the liquid into the sliced veggies. Note: this requires some strength and persistence. Make sure that liquid covers the solid food particles. Cover jar with cloth to allow it to breathe. Ferment for 2–3 days at room temperature. After 2–3 days, place jar in refrigerator to stop fermentation process. Yields 1 gallon.

RAW FAMILY'S FAMOUS
RAW-SSIAN PICKLES

3   pounds pickling cucumbers
½   big bunch pickling dill (with seeds)
4   horseradish leaves (for crunchiness)
1   medium head garlic
6   cups water
9   tablespoons sea salt

Cut ¼ inch off both ends of pickling cucumbers. Stuff the
cucumbers into a glass gallon jar with garlic, dill (with seeds),
and fresh horseradish leaves. If you have a hard time finding
horseradish leaves, you may use grape, currant, or cherry leaves
instead. Mix the water and salt in a blender. Pour the saltwater
into the glass gallon jar to cover the pickles. If necessary, add plain
water to completely submerge the pickles. Let this jar sit out on the
counter covered with a cloth for 2 days. On day 3, the pickles will
be ready to eat. If you decide after 4 or 5 days that you want them
to stop pickling, drain the water, cover the jar with a lid, and place
it in the refrigerator. The salt acts as a preservative and keeps the
pickles from going bad. They can stay in your refrigerator for up to
3 weeks. If you prefer not to consume such large amounts of salt,
simply soak a few of the pickles in fresh water for a couple of hours
before eating them. The fresh water will pull the salt right out.
Yields 1 gallon.

LIVE KIMCHI

3   heads Napa cabbage
3   cups water
5   tablespoons dried paprika powder

6	large cloves garlic
10	Medjool dates
1	3-inch-long piece ginger
3	tablespoons salt
¼	cup lemon juice
3	hot peppers
1	packet vegan kefir starter

Slice cabbage into moderately thin strips, approximately ¼-inch wide, and stuff into a glass gallon jar. Keep in mind that the cabbage shrinks quite a bit as it ferments, so really pack it in. Blend remaining ingredients for 1 minute until smooth, and pour into gallon jar, completely submerging the cabbage. Shake the jar to ensure that the marinade sauce reaches all areas of the jar. If necessary, press down firmly on the cabbage to cover it with the marinade. Fill a glass quart jar with water and place it on top of the kimchi inside the gallon jar to keep the cabbage submerged. Cover the gallon jar with a cloth. Leave kimchi under this press on your counter for 12–24 hours and then refrigerate. Yields 1 gallon.

MISO MUSHROOMS

½	pound white mushrooms, sliced
2	tablespoons chickpea miso
1	tablespoon coconut oil
¼	cup water
5	sprigs fresh oregano, diced
1	lemon, juiced

Slice mushrooms and place into a bowl. In a blender, process the remaining ingredients. Pour marinade over mushrooms and let marinate for 15–20 minutes. Serve with your favorite raw entrée. Serves 2–3.

MARINATED DRIED MUSHROOMS

Sergei absolutely prefers this method of marinating mushrooms to any other.

3–4 cups dehydrated mushrooms
1½ cups Nama Shoyu
2 tablespoons olive oil
¼ cup lemon juice
1 pinkie-sized piece ginger, peeled and diced
2–3 tablespoons honey
1–2 teaspoons sea salt

Place dried mushrooms in a deep bowl or glass jar. Blend the remaining ingredients in blender until smooth. Pour blender content over mushrooms and mix so that all mushrooms are soaked. Soak for 3–5 hours. Dice a little green onion or chile pepper and sprinkle over mushrooms before serving. Use as side dish or mix into salad. Serves 7–9.

MARINATED MUSHROOMS

1–2 pounds chopped shitake, crimini, or button mushrooms
½ cup lemon juice
1 tablespoon honey
1 bunch fresh basil
½ cup olive oil
1–2 tablespoons sea salt
1 cup water
1 chile pepper

Place mushrooms in a deep bowl or glass jar. Blend the remaining ingredients in blender until smooth. Pour blender content over mushrooms and mix so that all mushrooms are soaked. Soak for 3–5 hours. Dice a little green onion or chile pepper and sprinkle over mushrooms before serving. Use as side dish or mix into salad. Yields 1 gallon.

CULTURED VEGGIES

1	red cabbage
1	green cabbage
1	celeriac
3	carrots
1	large beet
1	parsnip
3	cups water
6	large cloves garlic
3	hot peppers
3	tablespoons salt
1	small bag vegan kefir

Using the grating and slicing attachments on your food processor, grate and slice the first 6 ingredients and pack them into a gallon jar. Blend the remaining ingredients for the marinade. Pour marinade over the vegetables in the jar. Blend ingredients for 1 minute until smooth, and pour into gallon jar, completely submerging the veggies. Shake the jar to ensure that the marinade reaches all areas of the jar. If necessary, press down firmly on the cabbage to cover it with the marinade. Fill a glass quart jar with water and place it on top of the shredded veggies inside the gallon jar to keep them submerged. Cover the gallon jar with a cloth. Leave veggies under this press on your counter for 12–24 hours and then refrigerate. Yields 1 gallon.

SIX

Travel Foods & Wild Edibles

Trail Mixes and Dried Soups

Trail mixes serve several valuable purposes. Not only are they easy to mix but easy to transport and socially accepted. While we enjoy looking freakish carrying around a jar of green goop at all times, many do not share this enthusiasm. When you are hungry for a snack on the go, it can be a lot easier to indulge in a handful of trail mix, which most people are accustomed to seeing. We find that, when conducting business-related errands with people who do not share our joy for fresh foods, sticking to something seemingly ordinary helps us fit in better.

Trail mix is also a valuable food for hikers, because it offers satisfaction in a cute little package. When hiking all summer with his hiking company, Sergei always made a point of having a bag of trail mix on hand so that he could feed his customers as well as himself. Sergei's fellow hikers always complimented him on his mixes, noting that conventional mixes were so boring and that his were delectable.

The recipe for dried soup came to us when we were stuck inside an airport for over twenty hours with nothing to eat. We were so hungry that we started visualizing various foods in hopes that they would miraculously land in our stomachs. While the actual food never materialized, the idea for a dehydrated soup was born. In this chapter, you will find only one recipe for dehydrated soup, an ever-shifting recipe that constantly changes due to vegetable availability. We invite you to try our recipe in your travels and then add your own twist to it. Since the birth of this dehydrated soup, we have never been hungry in an airport. When we eat this soup on airplanes, our fellow passengers turn their heads and asked the flight attendant if they can have what we are eating.

SPICED ALMONDS

1	pounds almonds, soaked overnight
6	cups distilled water
1	large tomato
1	habañero pepper
½	cup olive oil
¼	cup lemon juice
¼	teaspoons sea salt
¼	cup raw honey
1	large bunch fresh thyme
½	cup onion powder

Drain water from almonds. Blend water, tomato, habañero, olive oil, lemon juice, salt, and honey in the blender for 3 minutes or until smooth. Dice thyme. Add onion powder to almonds. Mix all ingredients together and leave to marinate for 3 hours. Spread out on dehydrator trays and dry for 18 hours at 110°. Yields 1 pound.

CRUNCHY SUNFLOWER SEEDS

1	pound sunflower seeds, soaked overnight
8	cups distilled water
1	cup balsamic vinegar
½	cups Nama Shoyu
1–2	teaspoons sea salt
1	habañero pepper
½	cup raw honey
1	large bunch fresh basil
½	cup onion powder

Drain water from sunflower seeds. Blend water, balsamic vinegar, Nama Shoyu, salt, habañero, and honey in the blender for 3 minutes or until smooth. Chop basil. Add onion powder to sunflower seeds. Mix all ingredients together and leave to marinate for 3 hours. Spread out on dehydrator trays and dry for 18 hours at 110°. Yields 1 pound.

CRISPY PUMPKIN SEEDS

1	pound pumpkin seeds, soaked overnight
8	cups distilled water
¼	cup lemon juice
¼	cup Nama Shoyu
1–2	teaspoons sea salt
½	cup raw honey
6	cloves garlic, minced
1	large bunch fresh thyme, chopped

Drain water from pumpkin seeds. Blend water, lemon juice, Nama Shoyu, salt, and honey in the blender for 3 minutes or until smooth. Mix all ingredients together and leave to marinate for 3 hours. Spread out on dehydrator trays and dry for 18 hours at 110°. Yields 1 pound.

SAVORY ALMONDS

5	cups almonds, soaked 8 hours
1	lemon, juiced
½	teaspoon sea salt
½	cup nutritional yeast
1	teaspoon poultry seasoning
3	tablespoons agave nectar

Mix all ingredients together and leave to marinate for 3 hours. Spread out on dehydrator trays and dry for 18 hours at 110°. Yields 2 pounds.

SWEET, SWEET ALMONDS

1	cup dried prunes, soaked in water 10 minutes
1	banana
1	pear
½	cup agave nectar
⅓	teaspoon sea salt
5	cups almonds, soaked 8 hours

Blend everything except the almonds in food processor until smooth. Mix almonds with liquified ingredients. Mix all ingredients together and leave to marinate for 3 hours. Spread out on dehydrator trays and dry for 18 hours at 110°. Yields 2 pounds.

ORANGE GREEN RED

3	cups shelled pistachios
1	cup goji berries
½	dried persimmons, chopped

Mix all ingredients together and take a hike! Yields 1 pound.

CASHEW-MULBERRY DELIGHT

4 cups cashews
1 cup golden dried mulberries

Mix both ingredients together and enjoy. Yields 1½ pounds.

BERRY GOOD TRAIL MIX

2 cups hazelnuts
1 cup pine nuts
1 cup pistachios
½ cup dried blueberries
½ cup dried cherries
½ cup dried mulberries

Mix both ingredients together and enjoy. Yields 2 pounds.

SEA CRUNCHY MIX

1 pound almonds
¼ pound dried sea palm (sea vegetable)

Mix both ingredients and enjoy on hikes, runs, or road trips. Yields 1 pound.

NORTHWEST MIX

3 cups almonds
½ cup dried tomatoes, chopped
½ cup dried onions, dried in rings
½ cup dulse flakes, chopped

Mix all ingredients together and enjoy. Yields 1 pound.

1	pound carrots, grated
4	red bell peppers, cored and chopped
1	pound mushrooms, sliced
1	large red or yellow onion, chopped
4	large tomatoes, chopped

Place chopped ingredients into a food dehydrator and dry until bone dry at 110°.

When dry, mix all veggies together in a jar or resealable bag. This is your travel soup! When you are ready to eat, sprinkle ½–1 cup of dried veggies into warm water. Add your choice of oil, salt, onion powder, or lemon juice for flavor. Allow soup to sit for 10–15 minutes before eating. Yields 1½ pounds of dry soup ingredients.

Breads, Crackers, and Chips

According to our surveys (polls and questionnaires administered in workshops and classes), breads and crackers are the hardest food for people to give up when striving to maintain a raw-food lifestyle. In Russia there is a saying: "As long as you have bread, you won't be hungry!" If you are new to raw foods, you are in luck, for we have spent the last fifteen years perfecting our bread and cracker recipes so that you won't have to give up such a delicious part of your diet!

CORNY CRACKERS

1,567	golden flaxseeds, or 2 cups, ground
2	ears corn, cut from cob
1	teaspoon ground cumin

½ teaspoon sea salt
1 tablespoon coconut oil
1 cup chopped tomatoes
¼ bunch dill

Mix ingredients thoroughly in a bowl and spread onto a dehydrator tray. Dry for 12–18 hours at 110°. Yields 25–30 crackers.

SWEET MANGO CHIPS

2 mangoes, peeled and chopped
¼ cup golden flaxseeds, ground
¼ cup cashews
2 tablespoons raw agave nectar

Blend ingredients in food processor. Spread onto dehydrator trays and dry for 10–12 hours at 110°. Yields 20–25 chips.

CHIPS

4 cups almond pulp (from "Almond Milk" recipe on page 151)
½ cup golden flaxseeds, ground
1 large tomato
½ lemon, juiced
1–2 cloves garlic
¼ bunch cilantro
½ teaspoon sea salt

Blend ingredients in food processor. Spread onto dehydrator trays and dry for 10–12 hours at 110°. Yields 25–30 chips.

CHIA SEED CRACKERS

3 cups chia seeds, soaked 8 hours
½ cup dried tomatoes
⅓ bunch fresh basil
3 cloves garlic
1 lemon, juiced
1 teaspoon sea salt
¼ cup raw agave nectar

Blend ingredients in food processor. Spread onto dehydrator trays and dry for 10–12 hours at 110°. Yields 25–30 crackers.

AMAZING CROUTONS

1 cup almond pulp (see "Almond Milk" recipe on page 151)
¼ golden flaxseed, ground
3 sprigs fresh oregano, diced
1 tablespoon onion powder
2 tablespoons olive oil
½ teaspoon sea salt

Mix all ingredients in a bowl. Add water or a juicy tomato if necessary. Spread onto dehydrator tray and shape into small squares. Dry for 6–8 hours at 100°. Add to your favorite salad or enjoy as snack. Yields 50–60 croutons.

CRUMMY CROUTONS

1 cup sunflower seeds, soaked 8 hours
1 cup almonds, soaked 8 hours
3 medium tomatoes
1 bunch green onions
½ bunch fresh dill

2   cloves garlic
2   tablespoons olive oil
1   tablespoon sea salt

Blend ingredients in food processor. Spread onto dehydrator trays and dry for 10–12 hours at 110°. Add to salads or eat plain. Yields 50–60 croutons.

GOLDEN FLAX CRACKERS

3   cups golden flaxseeds, ground
2   large red bell peppers
2–3 cloves garlic
¼   cup raisins
1   teaspoon sea salt
½   teaspoon ground cumin

Grind the flaxseeds in a Vita-Mix blender or coffee grinder and transfer into a bowl. Blend remaining ingredients in food processor and mix with flaxseeds. Spread mixture onto dehydrator trays and dry for 16–20 hours at 110°. Yields 18 crackers. See plate 10.

YELLOW FLAX BREAD

3   cups golden flaxseeds, ground
2   large yellow bell peppers, chopped
3   cloves garlic
¼   cup raisins
1   teaspoon sea salt
1   teaspoon ground cumin

Grind the flaxseeds in Vita-Mix blender or coffee grinder and transfer into a bowl. Blend remaining ingredients in food processor and mix with flaxseeds. Spread mixture onto dehydrator trays and dry for 16–20 hours at 110°. Yields 18 crackers.

RAW-SHIN PIROSHKIS

1   cup almonds
4   carrots, chopped
1   white onion, chopped
4   cloves garlic
½   bunch fresh dill, diced
½   spicy pepper
2–3   tablespoons olive oil
1½   teaspoons sea salt
2   cups flaxseeds, ground

Grind the flaxseeds in a Vita-Mix blender or coffee grinder and transfer into a bowl. Blend remaining ingredients in food processor and mix with flaxseeds. With an ice-cream scoop, scoop mixture onto dehydrator trays and dry for 18–20 hours at 110°. Yields approximately 12 piroshkis.

VALYA'S RAW BREAD

1   cup walnuts, soaked overnight
1   cup kamut, soaked overnight
1   large onion
1   cup ground flaxseeds
1   cup chopped celery
¼   cup olive oil
½   cup raisins
½   cup water
1   teaspoon salt
2   tablespoons coriander
½   lemon, juiced
2   teaspoons caraway seeds, ground

Blend soaked walnuts and kamut, along with the onion in the food processor until finely chopped. Transfer to a bowl and mix with the ground flaxseeds. Next, blend celery, olive oil, raisins, and water in a blender. Combine both mixtures. Add the salt, coriander, lemon juice, and caraway, and mix thoroughly. Shape the mixture into small loaves and place in dehydrator. Garnish loaves with crushed nuts or poppy seeds. Dry for about 24–36 hours at 110°. You may need to flip the bread after approximately 12–15 hours so that both sides dry evenly. Makes 4–5 small loaves.

IGOR'S CRACKERS

2	cups flaxseeds, ground in dry Vita-Mix container
1	cup water
1	large onion, chopped
3	stalks celery, chopped
4	cloves garlic
2	tomatoes
1	teaspoon caraway seeds
1	teaspoon coriander seeds
1	teaspoon sea salt

Grind the flaxseeds in a dry Vita-Mix container. Blend together remaining ingredients. Mix ground flaxseeds into blended mixture by hand. Dough consistency should be thick and sticky. Cover the dough with cheesecloth or a towel and let sit in a bowl at a warm room temperature overnight to ferment slightly. If a more sour taste is desired, ferment for up to 2 days. Using a spatula, spread on nonstick dehydrating sheets. Divide into squares of desired size. For softer bread, dehydrate for 16 hours on one side, 4 hours on the other. For crispy crackers, dry for 20 hours. Keep crackers refrigerated. Yields 18 crackers.

NORI CRACKERS

3   cups sunflower seeds, soaked 8 hours
4   stalks celery, chopped
1   large white onion, chopped
½   bunch fresh cilantro
3   cloves garlic
2   tablespoons olive oil
½   lemon, juiced
1   teaspoon sea salt

Blend all ingredients in food processor until smooth. Spread mixture on crispy sheets of nori and place in food dehydrator. Dry for 16–18 hours at 110°. Yields 18 crackers.

CORN CHIPS 1

4   cups corn
¼   cup olive oil
½   cup water
½   teaspoon salt
2   chile peppers
1   tablespoon honey
1   bunch cilantro
½   cup ground flaxseeds (use coffee grinder or Vita-Mix blender)

Mix all ingredients in blender except ground flaxseeds. Slowly add flaxseeds to mixture while mixing with a spoon. Spread onto dehydrator trays and dry for 15–18 hours at 110° or until crisp. Yields 25–30 chips.

CORN CHIPS 2

3   ears corn
½   lemon (with seeds removed)

¼	red onion
1	medium tomato
¼	teaspoon salt
3	tablespoons agave nectar
½	teaspoon Spike

Cut corn off the cob and place in blender along with other ingredients. Blend thoroughly. Use a teaspoon to transfer the mixture onto dehydrator trays in small, round puddles. Dry for 6 hours or until crunchy. Yields 25–30 chips.

SIMPLE CRACKERS

We like this recipe for both its simplicity and taste.

3	cups whole flaxseed, soaked 3 hours
1	cup water
½	teaspoon salt

Mix all ingredients and spread with a spatula on dehydrator sheets. Dehydrate for about 12 hours or until crisp. Yields 10–12 crackers.

RYE BREAD

2	cups sprouted rye
2	tomatoes
½	red onion
2	stalks celery
½	cup golden flaxseeds
⅓	teaspoon cumin powder
½	teaspoon salt
1	teaspoon honey

Blend ingredients thoroughly and spread blender contents onto dehydrator trays. Dry for 16 hours. Yields 2 loaves.

ZUCCHINI CHIPS

¼   cup Nama Shoyu
1   lemon (seeds removed to prevent bitterness)
1   clove garlic
1   1-inch piece ginger
1   tablespoon honey
4   thinly sliced zucchinis (yellow and green)

Blend first 5 ingredients thoroughly. Pour mixture over zucchini slices. Spread the chips out on a dehydrator tray and dry for 8 hours. Yields 100–150 chips.

CLOUD CHIPS

1   large tomato
1   cup almond milk
6   white button mushrooms
½   teaspoon turmeric powder
1   clove garlic
⅓   lemon
4   tablespoons Bragg Liquid Aminos

Blend thoroughly and spoon out onto dehydrator trays. Dry for 6 hours. Yields 25–30 chips. See plate 6.

YAM CHIPS

½   medium yam, peeled
½   cup golden flaxseeds
½   teaspoon sea salt
3   tablespoons agave nectar
1   clove garlic
⅓   teaspoon poultry seasoning

Blend thoroughly and spoon out onto dehydrator trays. Dry for 6 hours. Yields 25–30 chips.

POTATO CHIPS

5   medium potatoes, peeled
1   red onion, sliced
¼   cup olive oil
¼   cup lemon juice
½   teaspoon sea salt
½   teaspoon garlic powder
½   teaspoon onion powder
½   teaspoon paprika

Thinly slice potatoes and soak slices in water for 3 hours in a bowl. Drain water and mix in remaining ingredients. Spread chips out on dehydrator tray. Dry for 10 hours. Serves 5.

BANANA BREAD

2   cups almond milk
2   bananas
½   teaspoon vanilla
⅓   teaspoon pumpkin pie spice
1   tablespoon honey

Blend thoroughly and pour out onto dehydrator tray. Dry for 12 hours. Yields 6 pieces.

CORN BREAD

3   cobs corn
5   tablespoons agave nectar
½   cup golden flaxseeds
¼   teaspoon salt

Cut corn off cobs and blend in blender along with other ingredients. Dry for 12 hours. Yields 6 pieces.

CANDIED JICAMA

½ cup soaked dried apricots
1 banana
¼ teaspoon cinnamon
1 thinly sliced jicama

Blend apricots, banana, and cinnamon. Pour mixture over sliced jicama. Mix well and place on dehydrator trays. Dry for 12 hours. Yields 10 jicama strips.

JICAMA JERKY

⅓ cup dried tomatoes, presoaked 10 minutes
⅓ bunch cilantro
3 cloves garlic
6 tablespoons Bragg Liquid Aminos
1 sliced jicama

Blend dried tomatoes, cilantro, garlic, and Bragg's. Pour over sliced jicama and place onto dehydrator trays. Dry for 12 hours. Yields 10 jicama strips.

ALMOND BREAD CAKES

3 cups almond pulp (from almond milk)
1 medium tomato
1 carrot
½ bunch cilantro
½ lemon (seeds removed)
4 tablespoons Bragg Liquid Aminos

Blend thoroughly and spoon out onto dehydrator trays. Dry for 7 hours or until crunchy. Yields 25–30 cakes.

WILD EDIBLE RECIPES

This section presents a description of eleven of the most common wild edibles around the United States. At the end of each wild edible description, you will also find a fresh recipe that will drive you wild!

Wild Strawberry

Latin Name: *Fragaria virginiana*

Description: Wild strawberries grow near the ground in quaint patches. Each plant has one stem with three green leaves. Leaves are serrated with well-defined straight veins. Wild strawberry plants grow 2 to 8 inches tall.[1] Flowers are white and have five wide petals.

Habitat: Strawberries love the shade and can be found on mountain slopes and in forest settings. They thrive throughout North America.

Food Use: The red berries are delicious and can be eaten in many different ways. Strawberry greens are best when young. They can be used in salads or added to smoothies.

Nutrition: Rich in vitamins A, C, and K, as well as minerals sulfur, calcium, potassium, and iron, strawberries have been used to treat stomach upsets, diarrhea, urinary tract infections, and intestinal disorders. They have also proven to be beneficial for tightening the skin and closing pores.[2] (See plates 39 and 40.)

STRAWBERRY SUN TEA

1	pint freshly picked strawberries
1	bunch fresh mint
1	thumb-sized piece ginger, diced
2	tablespoons honey
1	lime, cut in half

Transfer all ingredients into a glass gallon jar. Cover all ingredients with water and secure lid on jar. Place jar in a sunny spot, preferably outdoors. Let the water absorb the fragrance for 8–12 hours. Serve chilled or with ice. Serves 4–6.

Chickweed

Latin Name: *Stellaria media*

Description: Chickweed is green in color and grows to 12 inches in height. Leaves have sharp tips and are arranged in pairs. The tiny flowers have five petals, are hued white, grow relatively sparse, and are found primarily at the top of the stem. The plant's weak stems often trail on the ground.

Habitat: Chickweed grows throughout the continental United States. It prefers moist, woodland areas. Chickweed is a common weed in gardens and in areas where soil has been disturbed.

Food Use: Chickweed is a tender, mild green. It can be eaten raw as a trailside nibble or can be added into a salad.

Nutrition: According to Janice J. Schofield, chickweed is known for soothing irritated tissues, aiding bladder, kidney, and urinary difficulties. When applied topically as a salve, chickweed eases burns, bug bites, cuts, and scrapes. Topical application is also great for fighting infections. (See plates 41 and 42.)

CHICKWEED SMOOTHIE

3½   cups freshly picked chickweed
½   bunch romaine lettuce
2   ripe pears
1   cup fresh apple juice
½   teaspoon cinnamon powder
½   cup ice cubs

Blend all ingredients in blender for 2 minutes or until thoroughly mixed. Pour into fancy glasses and serve. Serves 2–3.

Clover

Latin Name: *Trifolium repens*

Description: Clovers have round green leaves with whitish crescent-shaped prints. Leaves grow in groups of 3. Flowers range in color, have upwards of forty petals, and cluster together, creating an overall spherical shape.

Habitat: Clovers grow in fields, near roadways, lawns, waste areas, and sunny meadows in many places around the globe.

Food Use: Flowers and leaves can be eaten raw. The flowers have a sweet taste and make a delicious, colorful addition to any dish.

Nutrition: Clovers contain beta-carotene as well as vitamins C, B vitamins, biotin, choline, inositol, and bioflavonoids.[5] Clovers are rich in minerals such as magnesium, manganese, zinc, copper, and selenium. They are used for blood purification, cancer growths, hepatitis, and AIDs.[6] (See plate 43.)

Recipe Tip: Great decoration! Use clover flowers when decorating salads, pâtés, pies, cakes, drinks, sandwiches, and anything else.

CLOVER SALAD

2	cups fresh clover
1	cucumber
1	tomato
1	avocado
1	tablespoon lime
1	tablespoon olive oil
¼	teaspoon salt

Chop up vegetables and place in a bowl. Mix in remaining ingredients. Serves 2-3.

Dandelion

Latin Name: *Taraxacum officinale*

Description: Dandelions typically have sharply serrated green leaves resembling teeth. The French name for dandelion is *dent de lion*, which means "tooth of the lion." Dandelions have 1 yellow flower per stem. These flowers mature and become the white, puffy blow balls that many of us blew into the wind in childhood.

Habitat: Dandelions grow almost everywhere worldwide. They are often observed growing on lawns and roadways as well as in wild woodland settings.[7] Varieties of dandelions can be harvested in the desert, the tundra, and everywhere in between.

Food Use: Greens can be used in salads, smoothies, or as trailside nibbles.[8] Flowers can be eaten raw or made into jam. Roots can be eaten raw or dried and ground up for use as a coffee substitute.

Nutrition: Schofield writes that dandelion greens are "exceptionally high in vitamins A, B, and C, and the minerals copper, phosphorus, potassium, iron, calcium, and magnesium." The flowers are rich in vitamin D. Dandelions are widely used to treat obstructions of the liver, kidneys, gallbladder, pancreas, and spleen. Dandelion root contains insulin, which makes it favorable for diabetics.[9] (See plate 44.)

DANDELION-INFUSED HONEY

1   cup freshly picked dandelion flowers
1   cup raw honey

Rinse off flowers and trim excess stems. Place honey and flowers in a jar and mix thoroughly. Let the flowers soak up honey for 3 or more days. Spread as a jam on bread or crackers.

Lamb's-Quarter

Latin Name: *Chenopodium album*

Description: Lamb's-quarter can grow up to 10 feet tall. The plant has green, triangular leaves. Leaves are dusted with a whitish film, which rubs off when touched. Flowers are tiny and grow in the crown of the plant.

Habitat: Lamb's-quarter thrives as a common weed in gardens and also grows near streams, rivers, and forest clearings. Lamb's-quarter is widespread throughout the United States.

Food Use: Lamb's-quarter can be eaten raw in salads, smoothies, and juices, or as a trailside nibble. Leaves resemble spinach in taste and texture. One lamb's-quarter plant can produce up to 75,000 seeds.[10] The seeds, which resemble poppy seeds, are also a viable food source.

Nutrition: Lamb's-quarter is rich in protein; vitamins A and C; and the B vitamins thiamine, riboflavin, and niacin.[11] Plants have a high saturation of the minerals iron, calcium, phosphorus, and potassium. (See plate 45.)

LAMB'S-QUARTER SOUP

1	cup cashews
1	ripe tomato
1½	cups water
2–3	cloves garlic
1	teaspoon onion powder
½	lime, juiced
1	tablespoon olive oil
1	teaspoon agave nectar
½	teaspoon sea salt
1	cup freshly picked lamb's-quarter, chopped
½	medium avocado, chopped into cubes
½	red bell pepper, sliced into thin strips

Blend first 9 ingredients in blender for 3 minutes or until smooth. Add the remaining ingredients for texture. Mix ingredients into soup and serve. Garnish with wild-edible flowers such as nasturtiums. Serves 2–3.

Miner's Lettuce

Latin Name: *Claytonia perfoliata*

Description: Miner's lettuce is an annual plant that usually pops its head out in early spring. It is light green with round, disk-like leaves, which surround its smooth, tender stem. This stem, which passes directly through the round leaf, is a key identifier of miner's lettuce. After the plant has bloomed, a small white or pinkish flower grows atop its rounded leaves. Miner's lettuce ranges from 1 to 12 inches tall and may have anywhere from one to over twenty-five stems growing out of a single root.

Habitat: Miner's lettuce grows from Alaska down the West Coast to Baja, California, and east to Arizona, Utah, Colorado, Wyoming, and the Dakotas. It prefers cool, moist places, which means that it is most abundant in shady areas. It can grow up to six-thousand feet above sea level.

Food Use: The whole plant can be eaten raw in salads or as a trail nibble. Miner's lettuce is very mild, tender, and, most of all, delicious.

Nutrition: It is rich in vitamin C, which was used by early settlers to fight off scurvy. It also contains trace minerals. (See plate 46.)

MINER'S LETTUCE SALAD

4	cups miner's lettuce, chopped (use every part of plant)
½	cup basil, leaves pulled from the stem and used whole
¼	cup dried tomatoes, soaked 15 minutes
¼	cup pine nuts
1	tablespoon balsamic vinegar
1	tablespoon olive oil
½	teaspoon sea salt

Mix all ingredients in a bowl. Garnish with edible flowers and enjoy. Serves 3.

Plantain

Latin Name: *Plantago major*

Description: Plantain leaves can grow up to 1 foot long, ranging in shape from round- to lance-leafed. Leaves are of solid green pigment and have very defined parallel veins running up the underside. Plantain buds and flowers grow at the top of a long, narrow stem and bear slight resemblance to baby corn.

Habitat: Plantain is commonly found in sunny meadows and near roadways, lawns, waste areas, and other places where the soil has been disturbed. Various species of plantain grow throughout North America and Europe.

Food Use: Tender leaves can be used as salad greens. Buds and flowers can be marinated.[12]

Nutrition: Plantain provides beta-carotene and calcium. Its richness in fiber reduces low-density lipoproteins (LDL) cholesterol and triglycerides.[13] According to Rosemary Gladstar of the California School of Herbal Studies, plantain juice and poultices treat and reverse blood poisoning. Plantain is also famous for healing stings, burns, bites, abscesses, and infections.[14] (See plate 47.)

PLANTAIN COCKTAIL

1   bunch freshly picked plantain
3   apples, chopped
½   lime with peel
1   thumb-sized piece fresh ginger

Juice ingredients in juicer. Add ice cubes or chill before serving. Garnish with edible flowers. Serves 2.

Purslane

Latin Name: *Portulaca oleracea*

Description: Purslane leaves are paddle-shaped, are light-green colored, and have a reddish stem. The plant stem is smooth and succulent, and emits a slimy, okra-like juice when bent or broken. Hidden amid the leaves of the plant are tiny, yellow flowers with five petals.[15]

Habitat: Purslane loves sandy soils and therefore can be found in areas such as abandoned parking lots, fields, vacant lots, and other disturbed soils across the United States.

Food Use: Purslane is both tasty and nutritious. It has a slightly sour taste, which is pleasant for the palate. The whole plant can be eaten raw.

Nutrition: Purslane is rich in iron, beta-carotene, vitamin C, phosphorus, and riboflavin. It is a great source of omega-3 fatty acids, which prevent heart disease and improve immune system functions.[16] (See plate 48.)

PURSLANE SUMMER SOUP

1–2	cups freshly picked purslane (leaves and stems)
2	cups ripe farmers' market tomatoes
½	bunch fresh basil
½	habañero pepper
1	tablespoon olive oil
½	lemon, juiced
1	teaspoon raw honey
½	teaspoon sea salt
½	cup freshly picked purslane (leaves only)
1	medium carrot, grated
¼	cup soaked walnuts

Blend first 8 ingredients in blender for 3 minutes or until smooth. Add the remaining ingredients for texture. Garnish with olives and dried tomatoes. Serves 2–3.

Sheep Sorrel

Latin Name: *Rumex acetosella*

Description: Sheep Sorrel can vary from six inches to two feet tall. It has lance-shaped green leaves with two lobes that are easy to distinguish from other plants. Many people identifying sheep sorrel for the first time comment that its leaves resemble a fish or a sword. The flowers grow on the plant's elongated stock with colors ranging from white to red.

Habitat: Sorrel likes disturbed soil and is often found in empty fields, in rocky meadows, and along roadways. Sheep sorrel can be found throughout the continental United States.

Food Use: Leaves and flowers can be eaten raw in salads or as a trailside nibble. The tender leaves taste sour and make a lovely addition to smoothies or salad dressings. When crushed, added to water, and mixed with natural sweetener, sorrel leaves make a mouthwatering lemonade substitute when lemons are unavailable.

Nutrition: Sorrel is rich in iron and great for treating constipation, blood disorders, skin disease, rheumatism, and indigestion. It is also great for cleansing the system of heavy metals such as lead, arsenic, and mercury. (See plates 49 and 50.)

SHEEP SORREL LEMONADE

1   cup sheep sorrel leaves, crushed
2–3   cups water
2   tablespoons honey
1   pinch wild mint (optional)

Mix all ingredients. Serve after 15 minutes. Serves 3.

Stinging Nettle

Latin Name: *Urtica dioica*

Description: Stinging nettle is a green plant with finely serrated, heart-shaped leaves. Its small, greenish flowers grow in clusters and droop from its leaves. The nettle can grow up to 7 feet tall and is covered with tiny stinging hairs, which give the plant its name.

Habitat: Nettles prefer cool, moist places that get limited sun exposure. Plants can be found growing in thickets near forest clearings and alongside streams and rivers. They grow across North America, Europe, Asia, and Africa.

Food Use: The whole plant is edible, but it tastes best when young and under two feet tall. While it can be eaten raw, this can be uncomfortable because you are likely to get stung by one of its spines. The spines, which are believed to contain formic acid and histamine compounds, will irritate the skin upon contact. Traditionally, nettles have been steamed to avoid the stinging sensation, but blending the plant destroys its needles and enables consumption in raw form.

Nutrition: Nettles have been used for hundreds of years to treat arthritis and other joint problems. They have been shown to have anti-inflammatory properties and also lower blood sugar, calm allergies, and relax sore muscles. Nettles are particularly high in iron, making them beneficial for people suffering from anemia. Tea made from nettles makes a great hair rinse, promotes hair growth, and eliminates dandruff.

Fun Fact: The same chemical compound the nettle plant produces that causes irritation actually soothes the skin. If you are stung by stinging nettles, apply fresh stinging nettle juice to the irritated area to completely neutralize the itch. (See plate 51.)

STINGING NETTLE PESTO

½   cup stinging nettle leaves
½   cup pine nuts

2–3 cloves garlic
1 tablespoon olive oil
1 tablespoon lemon juice
½ teaspoon sea salt
¼ cup dried tomatoes (optional)

Blend nettles in blender to destroy spines. Add remaining ingredients and blend thoroughly. Add more oil or lemon juice if necessary. Serve as you would regular pesto, for example, on crackers, bread, or pasta. Serves 3.

Thimbleberry

Latin Name: *Rubus parviflorus*

Description: Grows in shrubs ranging from two to eight feet tall and forms dense thickets. Leaves have 3 to 5 lobes and closely resemble maple leaves. Thimbleberries have white flowers with 5 petals each. The berries are red and closely resemble raspberries except that their overall shape is flatter (as if a raspberry had been compressed).

Habitat: Thickets of thimbleberries grow in moist, wooded areas in the lower mountainous regions. They grow best in cool environments and therefore prefer shade. Thimbleberries can be found from the Alaska Panhandle all the way down to Southern California.

Food Use: The berries are edible and very delicious, with a sweet and nutty taste that is both unique and fragrant. The flowers are also edible and make a delicious addition to salads. Thimbleberry leaves can be used either fresh or dried in herbal teas.

Nutrition: Throughout history, thimbleberries have been used to treat intestinal ailments and upset stomachs. When roots are dried and prepared in tea form, they are great for diarrhea and dysentery. (See plate 52.)

THIMBLEBERRY SALAD

1   head romaine lettuce, chopped
1   navel orange, seeded and thinly sliced
½   pint freshly picked thimbleberries
¼   cup pine nuts

Mix all ingredients in a bowl. Garnish with edible flowers or colorful fruit.

DRESSING

2   tablespoons olive oil
1   tablespoon balsamic vinegar
1   teaspoon agave nectar
½   teaspoon sea salt

Thoroughly mix ingredients in a small bowl or jar, and pour over top of salad. Serves 2.

Glossary

agar agar. A gelatinous substance made from red algae (a type of seaweed) and used as a substitute for gelatin to thicken soups, jellies, ice creams, etc.

arame. A mild species of kelp (seaweed) know for its high content of calcium, iron, and iodine.

cayenne. A hot red chili pepper used to flavor dishes, often available in powdered form.

chili pepper. A type of hot fruit used as spice in culinary cuisine.

dulse flake. A type of red algae often used as a salt substitute. Dulse can by purchased either whole or in flakes and is best known for its delicious, mild taste.

durian. A large, spiky fruit grown in Southeast Asia. Durian is said to be the king of all fruits. With its intense smell, custardy texture, and delicate flavor, it lives up to the notion that "it is the fruit that smells like hell, but taste like heaven."

lemon zest. The outer colorful skin of the lemon fruit. It is gathered by gently grating outer parts of the lemon. Lemon zest is used to add that extra bit of flavor in gourmet cuisine.

Nama Shoyu. Brand name of our recommended raw substitute for soy sauce.

quince. A small, yellow fruit from Southeast Asia related to apples and pears. The quince has a strong pleasant aroma and can be used to add flavor to smoothies, salads, and desserts.

spicy pepper. Any type of pepper that is hot.

Spike. Brand of store-bought seasoning, including parsley, dill and over 25 other herbs and spices.

spirulina. Also known as "blue-green-algae" is a type of lake or sea algae often added to food because of its many health properties.

tahini. Seed butter made from sesame seeds.

yogurt culture packet. Good probiotic bacteria, which is added to yogurt mixtures to help kick start the fermentation process.

Sources

ONE: **RAW IMMERSION**

1. Marla Cone, "Of Polar Bears and Pollution," *Los Angeles Times*, June 19, 2003, www.ourstolenfuture.org/Commentary/News/2003/2003-0619-LAT-popsandbears.htm.

2. Marshall B. Rosenberg, *Nonviolent Communication, a Language of Life—Create Your Life, Your Relationships, and Your World in Harmony with Your Values*, 2nd ed. (Encinitas, Ca: PuddleDancer Press, 2003).

3. Saul Kassin, "Chapter 16: Psychological Disorders," *Psychology*, 3rd ed. (Upper Saddle River, NJ: Prentice Hall, Inc., 2001).

4. Ibid., "Chapter 13: Social Influences."

5. Ibid.

6. Hank Boschen, "Aspirin Side Effects Include Death," juiceguy.com/ASPIRIN-side-effects-include-DEATH.shtml.

7. *Merriam-Webster OnLine*, s.v. "Relationship," mw1.merriam-webster.com/dictionary/relationship.

8. See Note 4.

9. Nutrasanus, Dandelion Root Benefits and Information, Monroe, GA www.nutrasanus.com/dandelion.html

10. Alfie Kohn, *Punished by Rewards: The Trouble with Gold Stars, Incentive Plans, A's, Praise, and Other Bribes* (Boston: Houghton Mifflin, 1993).

11. See Note 9.

12. J. Krishnamurti, *Education and the Significance of Life*, 1st ed. (San Francisco: HarperOne, 1981).

13. *Wikipedia: The Free Encyclopedia*, s.v. "Olfactory receptor neuron," en.wikipedia.org/wiki/Olfactory_receptor_neuron.

14. Better Health Channel: Healthier Living, Online, "Taste Buds Explained," www.betterhealth.vic.gov.au/bhcv2/bhcarticles.nsf/pages/Tongue?Open (accessed August 5, 2007).

15. Your Family Doctor, Healthy Food! "Your Food Addiction Is Great for Business," www.online-ambulance.com/articles/doc/o/grp/Healthy/pg/1/art/Your_addict.htm.

16. James T. Ehler, The Food Reference Website, "Watermelon," www.foodreference.com/html/artwatermelon.html.

17. *Medline Plus Medical Encyclopedia*, s.v. "Vitamin A," www.nlm.nih.gov/medlineplus/ency/article/002400.htm (accessed January 1, 2007).

18. Byron Katie, *I Need Your Love: Is That True?—How to Stop Seeking Love, Approval, and Appreciation and Start Finding Them Instead* (New York: Random House, Inc., 2003).

19. ———, *A Thousand Names for Joy: Living in Harmony with the Way Things Are* (New York: Harmony Books, 2007).

20. Myron Winick, *The Fiber Prescription* (New York: Ballantine Books, 1992).

21. Sourced from www.healthcastle.com.

22. United States Department of Agriculture, www.usda.gov/wps/portal/usdahome.

23. American Heart Association, www.americanheart.com.

24. Loyola University of New Orleans, www.loyno.edu/~ecoinst/ccfm/recipes/ArugulatoZucchini/CollardGreens.html.

25. en.wikipedia.org/wiki/Chlorophyll.

26. Victoria Boutenko, *Green for Life* (Ashland, OR: Raw Family Publishing, 2005).

27. See Note 25.

28. T. Colin Campbell and Thomas M. Campbell II, *The China Study: The Most Comprehensive Study of Nutrition Ever Conducted and the Startling Implications for Diet, Weight Loss, and Long-term Health* (Dallas: BenBella Books, 2006), 29.

29. Ibid.

30. Ibid., 31.

31. Bernard Jensen, *The Healing Power of Chlorophyll from Plant Life*, (Escondido, CA: Bernard Jensen Enterprises, 1984).

32. Richard Louv, *Last Child in the Woods: Saving Our Children from Nature-Deficit Disorder* (Chapel Hill, NC: Algonquin Books, 2006).

33. Janice J. Schofield, *Discovering Wild Plants: Alaska, Western Canada, the Northwest* (Portland, OR: Alaska Northwest Books, 2003).

34. Introduced Species Summary Project, "Dandelion *(Taraxacum officinale),*" Columbia University, www.columbia.edu/itc/cerc/danoffburg/invasion_bio/inv_spp_summ/Taraxum_officinale.htm.

35. Thomas S. Elias and Peter A. Dykeman, *Edible Wild Plants: A North American Field Guide* (New York: Sterling Publishing Co., Inc., 1990).

36. Daniel Moerman, *Native American Ethnobotany* (Portland, OR: Timber Press, Inc., 1998).

37. Sourced from www.vitamix.com.

TWO: **SAVORY DISHES**

1. Documentary film, *Raw for Thirty Days*, www.rawfor30days.com.

FIVE: **MARINATED AND FERMENTED FOODS**

1. Bernard Jensen, *Tissue Cleansing Through Bowel Management*, 10th ed. (Escondido, CA: Bernard Jensen Publisher, 1981).

SIX: **TRAVEL FOODS AND WILD EDIBLES**

1. Janice J. Schofield, *Discovering Wild Plants: Alaska, Western Canada, the Northwest* (Portland, OR: Alaska Northwest Books, 2003).

2. Steve Brill and Evelyn Dean, *Identifying and Harvesting Edibles and Medicinal Plants in Wild (and Not So Wild) Places* (New York: HarperCollins Publishers, Inc., 1994).

3. Brigitte Mars, *The Desktop Guide to Herbal Medicine: The Ultimate Multidisciplinary Reference to the Amazing Realm of Healing Plants in a Quick-Study, One-Stop Guide* (Laguna Beach, CA: Basic Health Publications, Inc., 2007).

4. See Note 1.

5. See Note 2.

6. See Note 1.

7. See Note 1.

8. Thomas S. Elias and Peter A. Dykeman, *Edible Wild Plants: A North American Field Guide* (New York: Sterling Publishing Co., Inc., 1990).

9. See Note 1.

10. See Note 2.

11. See Note 1.

12. Lee Allen Peterson, *A Field Guide to Edible Wild Plants: Eastern and Central North America* (New York: Houghton Mifflin Company, 1977).

13. See Note 2.

14. See Note 3.

15. See Note 12.

16. See Note 2.

Bibliography

Boutenko, Victoria. *Green for Life*. Ashland, OR: Raw Family Publishing, 2005.

——. *Twelve Steps to Raw Foods: How to End Your Dependency on Cooked Food*. Berkeley: North Atlantic Books, 2007.

Brill, Steve. *Identifying and Harvesting Edibles and Medicinal Plants in Wild (and Not So Wild) Places*. New York: HarperCollins Publishers, Inc., 1994.

Campbell, T. Colin, and Thomas M. Campbell II. *The China Study: The Most Comprehensive Study of Nutrition Ever Conducted and the Startling Implications for Diet, Weight Loss*, Dallas: BenBella Books, 2006.

Elias, Thomas S., and Peter A. Dykeman. *Edible Wild Plants: A North American Field Guide*. New York: Sterling Publishing Co., Inc., 1990.

Kassin, Saul. *Psychology* (3rd ed.). Upper Saddle River, New Jersey: Prentice-Hall, 2001.

Katie, Byron. *A Thousand Names for Joy: Living in Harmony with the Way Things Are*. New York: Harmony Books, 2007.

——. *I Need Your Love: Is That True?—How to Stop Seeking Love, Approval, and Appreciation and Start Finding Them Instead*. New York: Random House, Inc., 2003.

——. *Loving What Is: Four Questions that Can Change Your Life*. New York: Three Rivers Press, 2003.

Kohn, Alfie. *The Brighter Side of Human Nature: Altruism and Empathy in Everyday Life.* New York: Basic Books, 1992.

———. *Punished by Rewards: The Trouble with Gold Stars, Incentive Plans, As Praise, and Other Bribes.* New York: Houghton Mifflin Company, 1993.

Mabey, Richard. *Food for Free.* London: HarperCollins Publishers, 2007.

Mars, Brigitte. *The Desktop Guide to Herbal Medicine: The Ultimate Multidisciplinary Reference to the Amazing Realm of Healing Plants in a Quick-Study, One-Stop Guide.* Laguna Beach, CA: Basic Health Publications, Inc., 2007.

Moerman, Daniel E. *Native American Ethnobotany.* Portland, OR: Timber Press, Inc., 1998.

Peterson, Lee Allen. *A Field Guide to Edible Wild Plants: Eastern and Central North America.* Houghton Mifflin Company, New York, 1977.

Robbins, John. *Diet for a New America.* Walpole, NH: Stillpoint Publishing, 1987.

Rosenberg, Marshall B. *Nonviolent Communication: A Language of Life— Create Your Life, Your Relationships, and Your World in Harmony with Your Values,* 2nd ed. Encinitas, CA: PuddleDancer Press, 2003.

———. *Life-Enriching Education: Nonviolent Communication Helps Schools Improve Performance, Reduce Conflict, and Enhance Relationships.* Encinitas, CA: PuddleDancer Press, 2003.

Schofield, Janice J. *Discovering Wild Plants: Alaska, Western Canada, the Northwest.* Portland, OR: Alaska Northwest Books, 2003.

Thayer, Sam. *The Forager's Harvest: A Guide to Identifying, Harvesting, and Preparing Edible Wild Plants.* Ogema, WI: Forager's Harvest, 2006.

Winick, Myron. *The Fiber Prescription.* New York: Ballantine Books, 1992.

Index